JOB

JOB

A NEW TRANSLATION

EDWARD L. GREENSTEIN

Yale UNIVERSITY PRESS

New Haven and London

Published with assistance from the Louis Stern Memorial Fund.

Yale University Press books may be purchased in quantity for educational,
business, or promotional use. For information, please e-mail sales.press@yale.
edu (U.S. office) or sales@yaleup.co.uk (U.K. office).

Designed by Mary Valencia.
Set in Minion type by Integrated Publishing Solutions,
Grand Rapids, Michigan.
Printed in the United States of America.

Library of Congress Control Number: 2019932366
ISBN 978-0-300-16234-9 (hardcover : alk. paper)

A catalogue record for this book is available from the British Library.

This paper meets the requirements of ANSI/NISO Z39.48-1992
(Permanence of Paper).

10 9 8 7 6 5 4 3 2 1

A human, born of woman,
Is short of days and sated with restlessness.
He sprouts like a flower and withers.
He flees like a shadow and does not stay.

—Job 14:1–2

This work is dedicated to the memory of my students
who passed on well before their time.
Thomas Lichtman
Ran Zohar
Matthew Eisenfeld
Seth Brody
Richard Thaler
Zvia Ginor
Cynthia Culpeper
Alan Lew
Daniel Wagner
Joel Wasser
Ellen Singer
Rami Wernick
Yaakov Thompson
Thea Friedman
Evan Jaffe
Ilana Sasson

Whom the gods love dies young.
—ancient Greek epigram

Contents

Contents

Preface

I often begin a course or lecture on the biblical book of Job with a well-known quip: in the book of Psalms there is no connection between one chapter and the next; in the book of Proverbs there is no connection between one verse and the next; in the book of Job there is no connection between one word and the next. Although there is not a little whimsy in the last assertion, there inheres in it a certain grain of truth. The Hebrew of Job, with its eccentric idiom and often inscrutable text, poses an extraordinary challenge to the scholar of difficult language, the philologist, the lover of words.

For over a half a century I have been honing my skills as an interpreter of biblical and other ancient Semitic languages and literatures, publishing academic studies and brief commentary on the book of Job. With the publication of this annotated translation, I share with the reader a fresh reading of the text, drawing on decades of research and close study. My understanding often differs from current translations and commentaries on some of the larger questions and on many details. Although this translation is far from a full commentary, in the accompanying notes I seek, on the one hand, to explicate certain expressions and images and, on the other, to justify the philological choices and suggestions I have made. I have attempted to find an explanation for every word, phrase, and syntactic construction. With all due modesty, I believe this is more than most other translators can claim. Such work requires tremendous patience and effort. The most fundamental principle I have learned and adopted from my best teachers is that ancient texts at one time made good sense. My foremost aim in writing this translation is to make good sense of the text of Job, with all the limitations that are entailed. I have tried to achieve this goal while at the same time trying to reproduce in some form many of the poetic tropes that characterize the work.

My interest in the issues of the book of Job harks back to my freshman year in college, when I was caught up in the problem of evil—how can a good God allow innocent suffering?—during a course on the philosophy of religion. My fascination with the linguistic and poetic intricacies of the Hebrew text of Job began with an intense and in-depth yearlong course on that book at the Jewish Theological Seminary in New York with Professor H. L. Ginsberg, of blessed memory, who sought to work out every philological and interpretative problem in this most difficult of biblical texts. Ginsberg's class notes, some of which I could fully understand only years later, formed the foundation of my own investigations into Job. When a small fire broke out on the roof of my house some time ago, the first possession I took pains to remove was my notebook containing Ginsberg's insights and the many annotations I had added since taking his class in 1972–73. Several of what I regard as my best contributions to the interpretation of the language and discourse of Job I owe to Professor Ginsberg's genius.

Having taught the book of Job in one form or another for over four decades and having presented papers and lectures on Job at numerous conferences and in other academic venues, I am very beholden to many students and colleagues, who have provided me with ideas, feedback, and materials. I can hardly remember, much less

thank, them all. I would nevertheless like to express special appreci-
ation to Professors Michael V. Fox, Ellen van Wolde, Konrad Schmid,
Leong Seow, Carol Newsom, Marc Z. Brettler, Adele Berlin, Steven
Weitzman, Alexander Rofé, Peter Machinist, Mordecai A. Friedman, Noam Mizrahi, Scott Jones, Ken Brown, André Lemaire; and
to Dr. Uri Melammed, Dr. Takayoshi Oshima, Dr. Jeremy Pfeffer,
and Dr. Nissim Amzalleg. My research on Job has enjoyed support
from the Abbell Research Fund of the Jewish Theological Seminary,
Beit Shalom Japan, the Herzl Institute, and Bar-Ilan University. I
have benefited from the research assistance of several former doc-
toral students and, especially in connection with Job, from Dr. Dom-
inick Hernandez and Dr. Adi Marili. My student Kristina Toshkina
has afforded me the benefit of her expertise in Arabic. For some
technical assistance I am grateful to Ben Bokser.

My endeavors in biblical translation have been inspired by the
exemplary work of Professor Everett Fox the preeminent translator
of Biblical Hebrew prose. For several years I assisted Everett as a
first reader and consultant; I hope he will appreciate that some of
his method and sensitivity has rubbed off on me for the better. I am
grateful, too, to Professor Mark J. Mirsky, who in 1990 commis-
sioned and published in *Fiction* magazine my translation of the book
of Esther. His constant encouragement has meant much.

I am extremely grateful to Yale University Press for accepting my
proposal to publish a new and different translation of Job. It was
Professor Ivan G. Marcus who, having heard a series of lectures he
arranged for me at Yale in 2008, brought my project to the attention
of Jonathan Brent, at that time the editorial director. Since then it
has been Jennifer Banks who has shown interest, encouragement,
and exceeding patience in awaiting and receiving my manuscript. I
thank her and her assistant, Heather Gold, as well as the production
editor, Susan Laity, for seeing this book through the press. Lawrence
Kenney has been a wonderful copyeditor. I am also grateful to the

readers to whom the Press assigned my manuscript for their very helpful observations.

My wish is that this new translation will make a difference in the way the inspired and inspiring book of Job is read. In short, the work is not mainly about what you thought it was; it is more subversive than you imagined; and it ends in a manner that glorifies the best in human values.

A Note on the Transcription of Hebrew and Other Semitic Languages

Two broad audiences are anticipated for this work. One is a general audience, for whom technical aspects of transcribing Hebrew and other Semitic languages are of limited importance. The other is an audience with a great interest in information about Hebrew and other foreign words that are adduced for purposes of explanation and justification. I have therefore chosen a middle path: sufficient information is provided to the specialist, while keeping the transcription on a nontechnical level amenable to the general reader. Such a reader may be interested in transcriptions in order to see how similar one word is to another, for example, in puns and assonance, or in assessing the plausibility of an emendation (a reading of a different word from the one in the received text, assumed to have been corrupted by scribal error or illegibility in the course of its transmission). The specialist will want to examine all suggestions of readings that differ from the traditional Hebrew text; evaluate proposed cognates from other Semitic languages; and compare terms and phrases in related passages. A minimally accurate transcription, one that does not distinguish similar-sounding consonants, such as *tet and taw;* one that does not routinely indicate vowel length; and one that does not differentiate the stop consonants (*b g d k p t*) from their spirantized correlates (*v gh dh kh ph th*) should be sufficient for the interested Hebraist.

For the sake of relative accuracy, the guttural *ḥ* is distinguished from *h*, and *'aleph* (') and *'ayin* (') are differentiated. The consonant *waw* is transcribed *w*, not *v*, in accordance with its ancient pronunciation. The cluster *ts* is used for Hebrew *tsade* and *sh* for *shin*. Certain fine distinctions in Arabic, such as *ḍ* in contrast to *d* and *ṣ* in contrast to *s*, are not made here. Specialists will find the requisite word.

A Note on (Not) Translating the Names of God

The book of Job was written by a Judean, a Jew, who refers to the deity in the narrative framework of the book by the Israelite name YHWH (read traditionally as 'Adonai, "My Lord"). Originally it may have meant "the One Who Is" or "the One Who Causes to Be." The name ceased to be pronounced around the time Job was composed, sometime in the Persian period.

The characters in the book, Job and his companions, are not Israelites but "Sons of Qedem"—Transjordanians. Allusions to the narratives about Israel's patriarchs and matriarchs place Job and his interlocutors in that era. As non-Israelites of an early period and, so far as we can tell, monotheists, Job and his companions refer to the deity by biblically attested names that are not specifically Israelite: El, Elohim, Eloah, and Shaddai. 'El is the generic term for a deity and when used as a proper name is identical with the name of the head of the Canaanite pantheon. Based on etymology, the name connotes power, not goodness, the way the English term "God" does. Accordingly, to use the term "God" to translate Hebrew 'El would produce an inaccurate impression. When speakers use the name El and its derivatives Elohim (plural) and Eloah (a secondary singular form, made by dropping the plural suffix on Elohim), they do not imply the deity's goodness but rather his power.

The name Shaddai, most commonly translated "the Almighty," is of uncertain origin but is most likely derived from an archaic term for "mountain" (namely, "the One of the Mountain") or from the word for a divine spirit or demon (*shed*) or from both. It is used especially in the book of Genesis, usually in combination with El (El Shaddai). In Job it occurs alone or in parallel with El or Eloah.

In order to avoid an excessive intrusion of modern associations and to preserve the apparent intentions of the poet to create an antique atmosphere, the names of God will not be translated into English equivalents.

Introduction

Why a new translation? I have two motives. The first is personal. I have been deeply engaged by the challenges of the book of Job—its themes, literary affiliations, language, and poetics—for over four decades. During this period I have struggled to set the text in the best Hebraic form that I can and to understand it as authentically as I can in as many layers of sense as I can reasonably construe. It has been said that "translation is the most intimate act of reading."[1] My translation project has demanded that I try to find meaning in every detail and nuance of the text. My efforts in this intimate endeavor have been profoundly rewarding, even though I know one could continue this pursuit for many lifetimes.

The second reason for producing a new translation is on the face of it altruistic—to set the record straight. The book of Job is sometimes touted as the world's greatest poem. I would hardly challenge that assessment. It is nonetheless a remarkable claim, considering that virtually no reader of the original Hebrew has ever felt satisfied at having understood the poem at the core of the book verse by verse;

---

1. Spivak, 180.

and that virtually no translator has got a satisfactory amount of it right.

The earliest translations of Job, into Aramaic and Greek, already exhibit diverse interpretations, often reading a Hebrew word or phrase that is different from the one we have received. The classical rabbis were conflicted about whether the story of Job was historical or fictitious and whether Job was fundamentally pious or blasphemous. Early Christian sources immortalized the patient Job of the prologue, seeing in him, as in the "suffering servant" of Isaiah 53, a prefiguration of Jesus, who, though innocent, suffered greatly and ultimately became a paragon of righteousness and model of divine blessing. Medieval Hebrew scholars made many original suggestions toward the elucidation of this or that word; but they were almost entirely wedded to the traditional text, and they virtually all interpreted the book in line with theologies and philosophies that comported with their own or those of their contemporaries. Early modern and modern translations tend to canonize these traditional understandings, assuming the book has been more or less correctly interpreted.

However, the meanings of many words and expressions in Job are based on guesswork. One is often hard-pressed to reconcile the language of the translations with the traditional Hebrew text. There is no delicate way to put it: much of what has passed as translation of Job is facile and fudged. Translators have for the most part recycled interpretations that had been adopted earlier, dispensing with the painstaking work of original philological investigation that might lead to new and proper understandings. Modern commentators have made use of the ancient translations, but these were themselves all too often in a quandary. Accordingly, traditional interpretations have often held sway, and translators have usually followed suit, imposing their notions of what the book of Job is presumed to be saying on their largely unsuspecting audiences. They have, for example, blunted Job's attack on the deity's justice and presupposed that Job—who has failed to receive the explanation of his suffering that is revealed to the audience in the book's prologue and has repeatedly expressed his determination to speak his mind—acquiesces to the deity's browbeating in the end. In this and in many less significant instances a less prejudiced, or different minded, approach produces the very opposite sense.

Job's response to the deity's lengthy lecture on his prowess as creator and sustainer of the world—and on Job's total lack of power and esoteric knowledge—is routinely interpreted as surrender. The verse (Job 42:6) has always stymied translators. The earliest translation, an Aramaic version found among the Dead Sea Scrolls at Qumran, interprets: "Therefore I am poured out and boiled up, and I will become dust."[2] The two verbs are parsed entirely differently from the way they are most often understood today. A typical modern translation of Job 42:6 is: "Therefore I despise myself (or: recant), / and repent in dust and ashes."

The first part of this translation is a stretch, and the second part turns out, after advanced investigation, to be highly improbable. The verb in the first clause (*ma'as*) is assumed to be transitive, in need of an object, and the translators supply that object, either explicitly or by implication. Concerning the widespread interpretation as "recant," it is an invention of the translator—no such usage is attested in ancient Hebrew. It assumes an implicit object, "words" or the like, but no such expression occurs with this sense.[3] Concerning the rendering "despise (myself)," the closest phrase one can find occurs in Job 9:21: "I'm fed up with (despise) my life." However, the verb in

---

2. Sokoloff, 101. The first verb is derived from *m-s-s* "to melt" and the second from *h-m-m* "to be hot."

3. "To reject (God's) words" is what does occur (1 Samuel 15:23, 26).

question does not need an object. It occurs intransitively in the sense of "I am fed up" in Job 7:16, where it is often rendered correctly. In other words, there is a very weak foundation in biblical parlance for the common rendering. It stems from the presumption of the translator that Job is repentant.

The second verb phrase, ordinarily rendered "I repent," has other well-known usages. An often overlooked one is "to take pity, have compassion" (for example, in Psalm 90:13). Those who translate "I repent" tend to render the following words literally: "on dust and ashes." They assume that in Biblical Hebrew one can say, "I am doing such and such (in the present case, repenting) in / on dust and ashes." The assumption is false. An extensive examination of all phrases relating to performing an act in the dust, on the earth, and the like shows that another verb is required: if Job were "repenting" or "regretting," he would have to be "sitting in / standing on / lying in / being in (and so forth) dust and ashes." No such complementary verb is found here. We ought therefore to adopt the same meaning for the phrase "dust and ashes" here that we find in its two other occurrences, one in the haggling between Abraham and God concerning the fate of Sodom and Gomorrah (Genesis 18:27), where the patriarch humbly presents himself as no more than "dust and ashes," and the other in Job's characterization of his abasement: "making me seem like dust and ashes" (Job 30:19). The phrase is used figuratively of the wretched human condition.

In this light, Job, in 42:6, is expressing defiance, not capitulation: "That is why I am fed up; / I take pity on 'dust and ashes!' (= humanity)."[4] I note as well that in the preceding verses Job is mimicking the deity's addresses to him from the storm (see there). Mimicry is the

---

4. Compare Curtis.

quintessence of parody.[5] Parodic as well is Job's assertion in 42:2: "you cannot be blocked from any scheme." Job is unmistakably alluding to the disdainful remark the deity makes about the builders of the Tower of Babel in Genesis 11:7: "they will not be blocked from anything they scheme to do." Consequently, Job is parodying God, not showing him respect. If God is all about power and not morality and justice, Job will not condone it through acceptance. This response may not accord with the image of a pious, Bontshe the Silent-type Job that most interpreters have wanted to find in this biblical book. However, Job's defiance, a product of his absolute integrity, is not the only radical or surprising feature of the book in the reading presented and defended here.

What Is the Book of Job?

The book of Job is a *Wunderkind*, a genius emerging out of the confluence of two literary streams. One is a tradition of ancient Near Eastern texts that deal with the plight and appeal of a pious— but not entirely innocent—sufferer. While several motifs and images are shared between these Near Eastern texts and the poem of Job, two works in particular display a structural similarity to the Hebrew masterpiece. The Babylonian "Theodicy" comprises an argument back and forth between a suffering man and his friend, who urges him to eschew a critique of divine justice and acknowledge the positive signs of providence all about him. The form of debate and the theme of theodicy (justifying the deity) certainly evoke a family resemblance to Job. A more piquant parallel to the structure of Job is the Egyptian tale "The Eloquent Peasant." A poor farmer is rail-

---

5. Dentith, 3.

roaded by a landowner who seeks to steal his pack animal and the meager goods he is transporting. The peasant defends his honor before a magistrate. The magistrate is so taken with the simple man's rhetoric that he selfishly defers giving him justice in order to hear the man speak again and again. Eventually, with the help of the gods, it seems, the case receives a favorable disposition. The fact that the peasant's poetic speeches are framed by a prose narrative makes this Egyptian work a close parallel to Job, even though the former deals with human injustice and the latter with God's.

The second literary tradition of which Job partakes is the classical Hebrew corpus, not only the so-called wisdom texts of the Bible, like Proverbs and some of the psalms, but works of narrative and prophecy as well. Of the Hebrew Bible's three wisdom books, Proverbs, Job, and Qohelet (Ecclesiastes), the latter two shake the pillars of conventional theology. The doctrine of just retribution (the good are rewarded, the bad are punished), which predominates in most biblical literature and is trumpeted in many formulations in Proverbs and some of the psalms is challenged and contradicted in Job and Qohelet. The most obvious way to illustrate this phenomenon is to cite the following verse from Proverbs 13:9: "The light of the righteous shines, / but the lamp of the wicked wanes." This traditional dogma is quoted almost verbatim and elaborated by one of Job's companions, Bildad (18:5–6): "The light of the wicked really does wane, / and the flame of his fire fails to glow; / the light goes dark in his habitation, / and his lamp goes out on him." Job directly undermines this dogma by asking rhetorically (21:17): "How often does the lamp of the wicked wane? / And their ruin overcome them?"

The Joban poet's reliance on the Hebrew literary tradition goes well beyond this sort of citation, however. The annotations to the translation below indicate many of the allusions and sources, but for the sake of an impression consider the following few examples. The portrayal of Job as a Transjordanian figure of the generations of Israel's earliest ancestors is drawn through allusions to the narratives and nomenclature of Genesis. The idea that Job could mount a lawsuit against the deity is entertained by Jeremiah (12:1). Job's railing against what he perceives to be the deity's indulgence of the wicked finds precedents in Jeremiah (for example, 12:1–2) and Habakkuk (chapter 1). The prophecies of Isaiah son of Amoz (Isaiah chapters 1–39) and the "Second Isaiah" (an anonymous prophet of the Babylonian exile, in Isaiah chapters 40–66) as well as those of Jeremiah, Hosea, Amos, and others provide the poet with a rich reservoir of vocabulary and phraseology.

The character Job is legendary, not an invention of the poet.[6] Job is mentioned together with Noah and a certain Danel in Ezekiel 14 (verses 14, 20) as three righteous heroes who, when the imminent catastrophe arrives, will be able to save themselves alone and not their families with them—as Noah had done in the great flood (Genesis 6–9). Considering the nexus among Job, Noah, and Danel, some aspects of an earlier legend of Job can be reconstructed.[7] Noah we know. Danel we have known since the 1930s, when a north Canaanite epic called "Aqhat," for Danel's son was discovered at the ancient site of Ugarit, on the north Syrian coast. The epic, written down around 1300 BCE, tells of a righteous judge, Danel, who is granted a son by the gods. A somewhat impudent young man, Aqhat is slain by a petulant goddess. There is reason to believe that in a final, missing part of the epic the son is revived for at least part of the year (perhaps the part when the Hunter constellation appears

---

6. There was a king of Ashtarot in the Transjordan in the fourteenth century BCE bearing the name Ayyabu, that is, Job. It is possible, but far from likely, that the legendary Job is based on this historical figure (see de Moor).

7. Compare Spiegel. Danel is mentioned in a Phoenician context in Ezekiel 28:3 as well. The name is consistently spelled differently from the namesake of the biblical book of Daniel, a young Judean exile in Babylon.

in the sky). The son's restoration would have resulted from the gods' sympathy for the righteous Danel's grief over losing him. Which brings us to Job. Like Noah and Danel, he is a righteous man among the gentiles. In the biblical book Job's ten children are killed at the outset and another ten children are given him when his ordeal is over. In line with the legendary pattern, the return of Job's children would have been predicated on the righteousness of their father.

The biblical book of Job has a distinctive structure. It opens and closes with a story, which, like all biblical narratives, is written in prose. The prologue relates the circumstances under which Job, a uniquely perfect individual, is afflicted by God, and the epilogue relates a rapprochement between the deity and Job upon which he receives another estate and family. In the prologue Job maintains his devotion to God in spite of a sudden turn in his fortunes: "Can we accept the good from Elohim and not accept the bad?" (2:10). But when three old friends come to console him on the loss of his children, it becomes clear that the conventional wisdom, by which God would do nothing unjust, is not up to the task. They have nothing to say. It would seem that Job has begun to reconsider his commitment to blind piety. He shatters the silence by cursing his birth and excoriating the deity for ushering people into a life of pain.

Job's discourse, formulated like all the speeches in Job and most in the Bible in verse, triggers well-intentioned responses from his companions, each of whom Job answers in turn. The pattern of disputation is cyclic: the companions speak in order, and Job's replies are for the most part lengthier. Job conducts two arguments in tandem: one with his friends, the other against God. In the second cycle Job's friends abandon their sympathy as they become convinced that the erstwhile paragon of piety has turned blasphemous. Job has meanwhile initiated a lawsuit against the deity as his only recourse for discovering the reasons for his afflictions—to compel the deity to testify.

The clashes on two fronts set the stage for the remaining structure of the book. At the end of the third cycle (from which a discourse by friend Zophar is missing), Job makes a lengthy forensic presentation. Job's strategy succeeds in eliciting a response from the deity. However, prior to the original book's closure, a fourth companion, Elihu, is introduced. This young man, whose presence is noted nowhere else in the book, anticipates the divine discourses but adds a number of points that he feels were insufficiently made by the first three friends and are absent from the deity's response. Even if, as most scholars think today, the Elihu chapters were added belatedly, they form part of the biblical book. Ironically, because Elihu's discourses are immediately followed by the divine speeches, one may get the impression that the deity, by seeming to omit Elihu's embellishments, is rejecting them. The God who speaks out of the storm in the end is far less concerned with justice and human refinement than the God represented by Elihu.

Topic and Theme

The divine discourse near the end of the book is divided in two, separated by a brief response of dissatisfaction by Job that seems to prompt the second speech. Job responds to the second speech as well (see above), and then, in a stunning turn, God speaks again—this time not to Job but to his companions. Twice he praises Job for speaking "in honesty" (42:7–8), unlike his friends. The companions had rehearsed traditional wisdom in spite of the reality confronting them. Job had sized up reality and revised his beliefs. We the readers know from the prologue that Job's afflictions derive from the deity's pride, not from some moral calculus. In the context of the full structure of the book this does not mean, as interpreters have usually thought, that Job took back his criticism. Rather, the remark focuses our attention on the theme of honest speech. The topic of the dialogues between Job and his friends may be the question of divine justice. But the theme of the book, the one that upon reflection has been highlighted all along, is the importance of proper speech—honesty in general and truth in God-talk in particular.

For one thing, the bulk of the book is and revolves around discourse—people, and then the deity, speaking. It is a drama of words. For another, the physicality of speech is underscored: "Job did not commit-a-sin with his lips" (2:10); "Job opened up his mouth and cursed" (3:1); "my speech is a garble (to you)" (6:3); "(How long) will the words of your mouth be a massive wind?" (8:2); and so forth. In the beginning Job's paramount concern is that his children did not sin by "blessing" (used here euphemistically of cursing) the deity "in their hearts" (1:5). The test of Job's piety is whether he will "bless" (curse) God or not. Job repeatedly insists that there is no "corruption on my tongue" (6:30); "I swear that my lips will speak nothing corrupt, / and my tongue will utter no deceit" (27:4). When his companion Eliphaz refuses to believe he has enjoyed a revelation from a holy spirit (4:12–21; see there), Job takes pride in the fact that, even if God were to slay him, "I did not conceal the words of the holy one" (6:10). Job is honest to a fault.

A corollary to the theme of integrity and honest speech is the conflict between Job's epistemology and that of his friends. The companions, as noted above, warrant their claims by appealing to traditional wisdom, sometimes in the form of pithy sayings. Knowledge for them is secondhand—what they have learned through the chain of tradition (see, for example, 8:8–12). Job demonstrates that he can quote—or invent—proverbial wisdom as well as they can (chapter 12). But he gets his insights from experience—from the implications he draws from the fact that he, a righteous man, sorely suffers; from a revelation, a particular experience, he receives from a rogue spirit (see the introduction to 4:12–21); and from the perennial sticking point that the wicked prosper. Job's companions seek to deny these claims, but Job perseveres in reiterating them.

The Historical Context and Language of the Book

Determining the time and place of the book's composition is bound up with the nature of the book's language. The Hebrew prose of the frame tale, notwithstanding many classic features, shows that it was composed in the post-Babylonian era (after 540 BCE).[8] The poetic core of the book is written in a highly literate and literary Hebrew, the eccentricities and occasional clumsiness of which suggest that Hebrew was a learned and not native language of the poet. The numerous words and grammatical shadings of Aramaic spread throughout the mainly Hebrew text of Job make a setting in the Persian era (approximately 540–330) fairly certain, for it was only in that period that Aramaic became a major language throughout the Levant. The poet depends on an audience that will pick up on subtle signs of Aramaic. A geographic setting in the land of Israel, in the Persian province of Yehud, is also fairly certain. The Transjordan is referred to as the East (*qedem*), and the Jordan River is mentioned in 40:23.

The author displays a familiarity with several Semitic languages— Phoenician, Arabic, and even Babylonian, in addition to Aramaic— and an acquaintance with local Canaanite mythology and some genres of Mesopotamian literature, such as the descriptions of gods (see at the Deity's Second Discourse) and incantations for the ease of childbirth (see at Job's Opening Discourse). Several words and expressions can be properly understood only when foreign languages

---

8. See Hurvitz, Joosten.

are brought into play. The poet appears to be a polymath whose knowledge of language, literature, and realia (animals, plants, law, astronomy, anatomy) is impressive. Most impressive, however, is his deep and wide familiarity with earlier works of Hebrew literature. He draws on numerous sources, and he dazzles like Shakespeare with unrivaled vocabulary and a penchant for linguistic innovation—in words, forms, and combinations.

The wide use of foreign, and particularly Aramaic, linguistic features in the poetic core serves distinct literary functions. On the one hand, the admixture of foreign words and sounds, together with the predominant Hebrew, yields additional possibilities for wordplay, assonance, and double entendre (see, for example, at 3:8). On the other hand, because the speakers in the book are Transjordanian, and to the east of Israel the Semitic idiom manifests many Aramaic features, the characteristic sprinkling of Aramaic colors the speech of the characters as dialectal, as foreign.

One may surmise that the poet who shaped the prose narrative and composed the bulk of the dialogues was an extremely well-educated Judean, probably living in Jerusalem, who was writing for an audience of like-minded intellectuals. The conclusion that the book was first written for a limited circle would also explain the sorts of difficulties that are posed by the text of Job.

Why Is the Text of Job Difficult?

There are several types of difficulty in the text of Job. One stems from the highly poetic vocabulary. The poet, as said, draws on language from a wealth of Hebrew sources. He delights in unusual meanings and forms. He also introduces, as said, foreign words and expressions, sometimes translated into Hebrew terms but often barely domesticated. Moreover, he occasionally invents Hebrew words, patterning them on known forms, adapting them to a particular need or fancy. Accordingly, the interpreter of Job must be alert to the possibilities and prepared to search for the word or form, in any available language, that makes the best sense of a passage.

For example, in 4:3–4 the first line in a set of four is routinely understood to convey Eliphaz's reminder to Job that he had always "taught the many" how to respond to a personal tragedy. That is the simple sense of the Hebrew (*yissarta rabbim*). This sense does not, however, comport with the next three lines, each of which highlights the support Job had shown the victims in physical terms: he would "strengthen" their "limp arms," "raise up" "the stumbling," and "stiffen" "buckling knees." A more physical manner of expression is expected for the first line as well. Such a meaning emerges when one realizes that the verb *yisser* has the unique sense of "fortifying" in Hosea 7:15 and that the word rendered "many" can with a minor change in vocalization be read as *rabim* (for *rabbim*) and derived from a Babylonian verb, used elsewhere in Job (33:19), meaning "to tremble."[9] The requisite sense can thereby be obtained: "It is you who have fortified the trembling." The commonplace translation of "teaching the many" becomes a secondary meaning.

Yet another kind of difficulty in reading Job is that a usage may depend on one's recognition of its source in order to understand it. When Job in his opening discourse (3:23) asks why light/life would be given "to a man/whose path is hidden" from the deity, nearly all translators misconstrue it. They interpret the first line to mean that the man's path is obscure to himself. The next line of the couplet they take to mean that the deity blocks the man's path from him. They entirely miss the point. The first line is drawn almost verbatim from Isaiah 40:27, where the sense is that people's path cannot be seen by the deity. The second line conveys therefore that it is God who

---

9. It is used in 4:14 as well; see there.

"screens (the man) off from (the deity's) sight"—and not that the deity puts an obstacle in the man's path.

There is another way to corroborate this interpretation. In many instances a later discourse in Job picks up on an idea articulated earlier. In this case Job alludes to it in 21:22 when he asks, "Can one teach awareness to El, / when he is judging from the heights?" The full sense of Job's meaning is brought out by Eliphaz in his elaboration in 22:13–14: "But you (Job) have said: 'What does El know? / Can he enact justice from behind foggy cloud? / The clouds are his blind, so he cannot see, / as he walks about the rim of the sky.'" Job wants to say that by remaining remote from the earth, the deity occludes his view of what happens to people. Job's intent would have been properly grasped had readers been attentive to the literary source of its language and / or the reiteration of the point later in the dialogues.

A final type of difficulty I will enumerate is that the poet employs language idiosyncratically to convey a technical meaning, such as a legal procedure or an eccentric notion. Perhaps the most outstanding example is Job's reference to the womb in which he gestated as his own. Whereas Job speaks of the "doors of my womb (belly)" (3:10), nearly all translators render it as the "doors of my mother's womb," even though there is nothing in the verse to suggest the presence of his mother. Not only does this interpretation suppress Job's perspective that the womb in which he wished he could have remained was his own—identifying with the fetus, Job does not know of or acknowledge that the space he inhabits belongs to another person. But by calling the womb his own Job establishes a key to the understanding of one of his later discourses. In his response to Bildad in the second cycle, Job painfully laments that his affliction has become a stigma from which the members of his family and society recoil. In delineating those who reject him, Job asserts the following: "My breath is foul to my wife, / and my odor to the sons of my belly" (literal rendering of 19:17). In the Hebrew and Aramaic of the Persian period the "son of one's belly" is one's child, and this is how virtually everyone (mis)translates it here. This sense is unsettling, however, because Job's children have all been killed in the prologue. Rather, once one recalls that Job's "belly / womb" is the one out of which he was born, one then realizes that the "sons of (Job's) womb" are the others who gestated there—his siblings. They, like his wife, keep their distance from him. The Joban poet sometimes creates a sort of private language; and the patient interpreter must discern it.

Job is wont to think differently, even surrealistically. When real life is unbearable, one may turn to the surreal. Job seeks to eliminate the day of his birth and the night of his conception after the fact; and he pursues a lawsuit against the deity. The latter is no metaphor, as many scholars describe it; the lawsuit is enacted and realized to the very end. Suing God may not seem real to the contemporary interpreter; but it is real to Job, to Elihu, who urges Job to drop the suit (34:23)—and to the deity, who responds.

The Problem of the Text and How to Resolve It

Not only are the language and rhetoric of Job a challenge, but the condition of the text is problematic. As suggested above, the book of Job probably circulated for a time within an elite circle. It did not begin as a sacred or traditional tract. There may not have been more than a few copies, if that. On account of the difficulty of reading and making sense of the work, scribes would have had a hard time preserving it properly and copying it correctly. When one inspects the early translations of the book, into Aramaic, Greek, and Latin, one is struck by how much they misunderstood (see the example from the early Aramaic translation presented near the beginning of this introduction). Specialists tend to agree that the ancient translators often resorted to guesswork, to the substitution of words they knew for words they did not, and to loose paraphrase. Scribes copying the original, too, often replaced unfamiliar words with more familiar ones, seeing what they felt more comfortable seeing.

Moreover, ancient scribes would often leave their mistakes uncorrected and move on. This means that if, for example, a scribe erred, omitting a verse or two, and only later realized his mistake, he would copy the omitted verses following the ones he got ahead of himself in copying. The result is that some verses are out of place. Another possible source of dislocation is that the pages of papyrus, on which Job or copies thereof were likely written, could come unglued accidentally or be taken apart for the purpose of interpolating another text. Scholars agree that several passages in the middle of the book (from chapters 24 through 28) are in partial disarray. I would explain this phenomenon by observing that toward the end of chapter 24 is a later insertion and that a roll of papyrus pages would have had to have been taken apart in order to insert the Elihu discourses, which include, I am convinced,[10] chapter 28 (see there). The separation of the earlier version of the text made for errors in the process of its reconstitution.

Be that as it may, part of the process of translating Job entails the reconstruction of the original arrangement of passages, to the extent that one can. There are several philological procedures one can apply in order to restore words and phrases as well as the proper sequence of the text. They all rest on the fundamental principle of making good sense in accord with the norms of the language, poetics, rhetoric, and logic of the ancient period. Our main guides are the texts of the Hebrew Bible and the extrabiblical literature from biblical times; and a careful examination of the structure, language,

---

10. So Clines, "The Fear of the Lord" and *Job 21–37*.

and rhetoric of the book of Job itself, in which certain patterns can be discerned. A foremost tool is the parallelism between two or more lines that characterizes biblical verse. If one line of a couplet is readily understood and the other is not, the clear line becomes a key to the form and meaning of the other (see, for example, at 4:2).[11] Sometimes we are assisted by the ancient versions, which may reflect a text that is more authentic than the one that has been preserved in the traditional Jewish scribal tradition (the Masorah).

The notes to the translation explain or at the least allude to the basis for restorations. Two rhetorical features of the poetry of Job are particularly helpful in this regard. One, as mentioned and briefly illustrated above, is the recapitulation or reiteration of a point in a later—or earlier—discourse.

Another and sometimes related rhetorical feature in Job that assists in the proper rearrangement of text is its dialogic character. Speakers relate to each other and often quote or paraphrase one another. Thus, for example, a passage in which the interlocutor is addressed in the singular must be spoken by one of the companions to Job. And a passage in which the interlocutors are addressed in the plural must be spoken by Job to the companions. Accordingly, a passage with a plural address within a discourse of one of the friends is almost certainly a quotation or paraphrase of Job. The most elaborate example of rearrangement in this translation is the reordering of sections in chapters 25 and 26, which in spite of the evidently secondary and mistaken attribution to Job in 26:1, is a single discourse, all belonging to Bildad. The first two verses of chapter 26 are addressed to a party in the singular; it is therefore Job who is addressed. Verse 26:4 asks the same addressee, whose words has he

---

11. This method will not always produce sure results, but experience shows that it usually will.

been revealing—an allusion to the speech of the rogue spirit that Job quoted in 4:17–19 and which is parodically paraphrased in 25:4–6. Once these pieces are lined up in order, the two other sections fall into place, forming Bildad's paean to divine grandeur; it starts in 25:2–3 and continues in 26:5 to the end. This is an easy enough jigsaw puzzle to solve.

In the course of the arguments, the speakers, as said above, tend to quote or paraphrase one another. Occasionally someone will be explicitly quoted; but that is the exception. Not to worry, however, there are some rhetorical cues by which we can identify quoted speech. The speaker may make use of a deictic (pointing) pronoun such as "this" or "these" as a preface to quotation. In producing a long series of wise sayings or mock proverbs in his first response to Zophar, Job precedes his citations with the rhetorical question, "And who doesn't have such (sayings) as these?" (12:3). Further, a switch from singular to plural may tip the reader off. When Bildad formulates his opening in the plural (18:2), it should be evident he is paraphrasing Job (in 16:3). In most instances of quotation the direct discourse will be introduced by references to speaking and / or hearing. Some obvious instances are in Bildad's first discourse (8:10) and in Eliphaz's paraphrase of the rogue spirit (15:13). Sensitive to these rhetorical cues, one should realize that 27:13–23, which do not sound like Job, are not from a misplaced speech of one of the companions, as many scholars propose. Rather, Job is citing the "nonsense" that his companions have been "spewing" (27:12). Explicit reference to speech can signal direct discourse. When a speaker gives a cue, we are meant to pick it up.

Most translators and even many modern interpreters of the book of Job are more interested in respecting the traditional Hebrew text than in restoring a more original one and in retrieving its more authentic meaning. One of the best of the modern commentators writes, for example, "Although [a particular] interpretation is somewhat strained, it has the advantage of reading the existing text."[12] From my perspective, there is no advantage at all to promoting an interpretation that is "strained," much less in translating a Hebrew that is gibberish. The diversity of ancient translations and interpretations demonstrates the frequent uncarty of both the text and understandings of it. The goal is to understand the text, not to sanctify it; and my assumption is that the text was meant to be intelligible—difficult but intelligible. A reconstructed text that is idiomatic, Jobian, plausible, and supported by analogous language elsewhere is certainly preferable to a received text that is simply impossible. If the object is to understand, then the philologist will take advantage of all available means to make sense. In view of what I have written above concerning the theme of Job—honesty in God-talk—it would be quite an irony indeed if one were to sacrifice intellectual honesty for piety in seeking to understand the book.

That being said, I have tended to reconstruct a sequence and correct a reading only when I felt it was necessary for a proper understanding. If one were to compare many modern commentaries on Job, one would find that my approach is, contrary perhaps to first impressions, fairly conservative. I try first to read the text as it is, and I believe I have often been able to explain the present language where others have not. To me it is nothing short of a miracle that a text as difficult as Job can be read and interpreted to such a large extent as received. By my measures, relatively little restoration has been needed.

A Word on Translation and on This Translation

Translation is not only interpretation; it is not only distortion; it is simplification. The act of translation ascribes sense not only to the

---

12. Hartley, 404.

intelligible but also to the barely intelligible and even to the unintelligible. It is nearly always easier to follow the translation of a poem than the original. The original enfolds within it untold levels of meaning and suggests a plethora of associations. The original purveys mystery in a way a translation rarely can. A translation necessarily transforms the opaque into the transparent. Accordingly, to read a translation of a book like Job is inestimably simpler than reading the Hebrew original. Even a properly restored Hebrew text is a formidable challenge, demanding that one turn time and again to the entire literary and linguistic resources on which it draws. No one can read Job without research, rumination, imagination, and speculation. The experience of reading a translation of Job, in which interpretative choices have already been made and served, cannot be compared to the exasperating grappling of the translator with the challenges of the Joban text.

And yet in the present translation of Job I propose a restoration and philological interpretation. I have made choices for the reader in line with my overall understanding of the arguments and of the particulars of language, rhetoric, and poetics. Although my primary objective is to convey an accurate sense of the original, I have attempted in addition to convey something of the text's poetics—its style, its imagery, its wordplays, its sound play, its rhythmic thrust, and the balance between lines. As any reader of literature knows, form and meaning go hand in hand.

My attention to rhythm and the sounds of the text is reflected in the translation of the prose narrative framework of the book as well. With the team of Martin Buber and Franz Rosenzweig and others as well as the tradition of chanting the Bible in the synagogue, I perceive a breaking of the prose sequence into rhythmic groupings, which Buber and Rosenzweig called "breathing units."[13] Although

---

13. See Greenstein, "Theories of Modern Bible Translation."

the text may have from the outset been written to be read, it is also engaging of the ear. The amount of alliteration, assonance, and punning one encounters confirms the oral nature of the text. As an added bonus, dividing the prose into divisions of unequal length, on the basis of syntax and sense, facilitates the reader's grasp of the structure and movement of the narrative and of the dialogue embedded within it.

Most translations of Job pay insufficient attention to the niceties of structure. To take a plain example: Job, in his opening discourse, lays a curse on the day of his birth and the night of his conception (3:3). He expresses this twofold pronouncement in two relatively balanced lines of a couplet. For reasons of syntax in the language of translation, most renderings divide the verse into three lines, thereby unraveling the intertwining of content and form. I have taken a small liberty, by repeating a word and reinforcing the pervasive sound play in the two halves of the verse, in order to produce a balanced couplet—one line for the day, one line for the night. I have tried to maintain a similar sensitivity to form throughout.

In the notes, if not in the translation I have made the reader aware of the way a notion is expressed in the Hebrew. Translations, as is well known, tend either to bring the source text to the reader in the reader's own idiom; or to bring the reader to the text and its world, exposing the reader to the thought and language patterns of the source culture. In this translation I have leaned toward the latter approach, believing it to be more authentic. It is certainly more in keeping with my primary philological purpose: to suggest what is actually being said in accord with the earliest established meanings.

JOB

PROLOGUE
(1:1–2:13)

The book of Job opens with a narrative in partly metered prose in which the deity, with the assistance of one of his angelic servants, the Satan, afflicts the pious Job over and over in order to see if he will maintain his piety or abandon it and "bless" (a euphemism for "curse") God. The figure of a pious sufferer is known in the ancient Near East, but there is no parallel there to the sort of test Job undergoes. The motif of testing a man by seeing how much pain he can endure is associated in folktales (from elsewhere) with measuring his devotion to a woman. And the Job narrative displays several features of a folktale, from the exposition (Once there was a man . . .) to the use of typological numbers (three, seven, ten). Taken together, these features suggest that God is testing Job in order to gauge the depth of his devotion, the bond of his love. Job withstands the assaults to his faith, but when three friends come to console him they have nothing to say, and it may be surmised that during the course of a week of silent sitting Job begins to reassess his beliefs.

The narrator refers to the deity by his Israelite name, YHWH, although he presents Job and his companions as "sons of Qedem," from east of the Jordan. The orientation is Israelite, but the setting is non-Israelite, suggesting a story of universal interest.

3

Prologue

[**1:1**] A man there was in the Land of Uts[1]—Job/Iyyob[2] was his name;
and that man was whole (in heart)[3] and straight (of path), and fearing of Elohim[4] and turning from evil.

[2–3] There were born to him seven sons and three daughters.[5]
His livestock[6] were seven thousand small-cattle[7] and three thousand camels and five hundred yoke of large-cattle and five hundred she-asses, and a very large servantry.[8]
That man was greater (in wealth)[9] than all the sons of Qedem.[10]

---

1. There may have been a locale of this name in northwestern Arabia, but the Hebrew name connotes counsel, wisdom—a land of the wise; see 1 Kings 5:10, where the legendary King Solomon's wisdom is compared with that of Qedem and Egypt. Uts is located in the southern Transjordan in Lamentations 4:21, where it is associated with Edom; and in Jeremiah 49:7 and Obadiah 8 Edom is noted for its wisdom.

2. The name is attested in the fourteenth century BCE as that of a Transjordanian ruler, Ayyabu. The name (in Akkadian) means "Where is (God) the Father?" but also connotes "enemy." Job will play on this latter meaning in 13:24.

3. See especially 1 Kings 9:4 and compare "pure of heart" (restored) in Job 36:5. But there is also a connotation of pure of path (see Job 4:6; 22:3; compare Psalm 13:6). Ironically, Job's illness will be represented by figures of disintegration, as physical wholeness will signify wellness; compare for example Psalm 38:4. Being whole in body ought to be the reward for someone who is whole in heart—a person of integrity.

4. More than simply piety, "fearing God" denotes a fundamental commitment to decency; compare Genesis 20:11; Exodus 1:17. See the Note on (Not) Translating the Names of God.

5. One cannot tell from the sequence of verbs whether Job's material prosperity followed or preceded his pious conduct—whether he was rewarded for his piety or whether it was coincidental.

6. The term "livestock" (*miqneh*) is associated with Israel's patriarchs; see especially Genesis 46:32.

7. Sheep and goats.

8. A rare collective term that in context alludes to Genesis 26:13–14 and other verses evoking the wealth of the Hebrew patriarchs. Job is depicted as a patriarchal type.

9. For *gadal* indicating wealth, see Genesis 24:35; 26:13; 1 Samuel 25:2; 2 Samuel 19:33.

10. Qedem, "the East," is identified with the area of Harran, the Hebrew patriarchs' homeland, in Genesis 29:1–4; see also Numbers 23:7; but here it may refer to the entire Transjordan.

[4–5] His sons would go about making a drinking-feast at the house of each on his birthday.[11]

They would send (messengers) and call for their three sisters, to eat and to drink with them.

When the days of a drinking-feast would come around, Job would send (messengers) to sanctify them;

And he would rise early in the morning[12] and offer up offerings in the number of them all,[13] for Job would say (to himself):

"Perhaps my children have sinned by 'blessing' (cursing)[14] Elohim in their hearts."[15]

Thus would Job do all the days.[16]

[6–8] On a (certain) day,[17] the sons of Elohim[18] came to station themselves around YHWH,[19] and the Satan[20] too came among them.

YHWH said to the Satan,

"Whence do you come?"

And the Satan answered YHWH:

---

11. Compare Pharaoh's birthday celebration (Genesis 40:20) and see Job 3:1.

12. Rising early evokes the Hebrew patriarchs; see for example Genesis 19:27; 20:8; 21:14; 22:3; 26:31; 28:18; 32:1.

13. That is, ten offerings.

14. "Blessing" is used as a euphemism for (God forbid) cursing God.

15. Not (God forbid) out loud.

16. On each of the children's celebrations; or every year, all the time (see 1 Samuel 1:21; 2:19).

17. For this usage, compare 1 Samuel 1:4.

18. Once denoting the lesser deities (Genesis 6:1–4), the term has come to mean the members of the divine court, the angels (compare Job 38:7).

19. The personal name of the God of Israel, traditionally rendered "the LORD." See the introductory comment to this section. The verb "to station oneself on" connotes service.

20. The Satan's role is to accuse and prosecute people for their transgressions. The title is derived from a term meaning "obstruction" (Numbers 22:32) or "opposition" (1 Samuel 29:4). The Satan seeks to trip up human beings and then report on their missteps; but he is also the contrarian, who contradicts the opinions of God.

"From roving the earth and from going all about it."[21]
YHWH said to the Satan:
"Have you set your mind[22] on my servant Job,
that there is none like him on earth—a man whole (in heart) and
    straight (of path), fearing of Elohim and turning from evil?"

[9–11] The Satan answered YHWH and said:
"Is it for nothing that Job is Elohim-fearing?
You have put a hedge around him and around his household and
    around all that is his.
You have blessed all that his hands do, so that his livestock[23] have
    waxed abundantly in the land.[24]
However—send forth your hand and affect[25] all that is his,
I swear[26] he will 'bless' (curse) you to your face!"

[12] YHWH said to the Satan:
"Here: all that is his is in your hand.
Just do not send forth your hand against him."[27]
The Satan took leave of YHWH.[28]

[13–15] On a (certain) day,[29] his[30] sons and his daughters were

---

21. The verb "rove" (*shut*) connotes spying (Zechariah 4:10) and is associated by
wordplay with the look-alike term *Satan*.
22. Literally, "your heart."
23. Some render "possessions," but when the term *miqneh* is not subjoined to another
term it refers only to cattle.
24. Compare Genesis 30:29–30.
25. Hebrew *naga'* has a strong connotation of affliction, plague.
26. A positive oath formula: "If X is not so (then may disaster befall me)."
27. Against him directly.
28. Literally, "went out from before the face of YHWH," from attending YHWH.
29. See above, verse 6.
30. Job's.

eating and drinking wine in the house of their brother, the
firstborn,
when a messenger[31] came to Job and said
"The cows were plowing and the she-asses grazing nearby them,
when Sheba[32] fell upon and took them
and the attendants they struck down by sword.
Just I alone have escaped to tell you."[33]

[16] While this one is speaking, this (other) one comes and says:[34]
"A fire of Elohim fell from the sky;[35]
it burned the small-cattle and the attendants, and it consumed
them.
Just I alone have escaped to tell you."

[17] While this one is speaking, this (other) one comes and says:
"Chaldeans[36] formed three columns,[37] and they swept over the
camels and took them;
and the attendants they struck down by sword.
Just I alone have escaped to tell you."

[18–19] While this one is speaking, this (other) one comes and says:
"Your sons and your daughters were eating and drinking wine in
the house of their brother, the firstborn

---

31. The Hebrew term can also denote a divine messenger, an angel (for example in 4:18).
32. A collective—the Sabeans; a south Arabian people whose famous queen paid a visit to King Solomon (1 Kings 10).
33. Compare the fugitive who reported to Abra(ha)m in Genesis 14:13; and see 1 Kings 18:22.
34. For the pattern, see 1 Kings 1:42.
35. Compare the divine fire from the sky (not necessary lightning) in 2 Kings 1:12.
36. A tribal people from Mesopotamia, attacking from the north.
37. Literally, "heads."

When here: a great wind came from across the desert;
it affected[38] the four corners of the house;
it fell on the young people[39] and they died.
Just I alone have escaped to tell you."

[20–21] Job arose; he tore his coat; he shaved his head;
he fell to the ground and prostrated himself.
He said: "Naked came I out of my mother's womb,
and naked will I return there.
YHWH has given, and YHWH has taken.
May the name of YHWH be blessed."[40]

[22] In spite of all this, Job did not commit-a-sin—
he did not speak insult[41] to Elohim.

[2:1–2] On a (certain) day, the sons of Elohim came to station
    themselves around YHWH,
and the Satan too came among them, to station themselves around
    YHWH.
YHWH said to the Satan:
"From where do you come?"
The Satan answered YHWH and said:
"From roving the earth and from going all about it."

---

38. See on 1:11 above.
39. "Young people" is the same word as "attendants" in verses 14, 16, and 17.
40. It is unusual that Job, a non-Israelite, refers to the deity by his Israelite name YHWH. The lines may be formulaic, placed without alteration by the narrator in the mouth of Job.
41. Compare Akkadian *tapiltu,* "unseemly speech."

Prologue

[3] YHWH said to the Satan:
"Have you set your mind on my servant Job,
that there is none like him on earth—
a man whole (in heart) and straight (of path), fearing of Elohim
    and turning from evil;
and he still holds-fast to his wholesomeness;
so that you have tempted me to devour him for nothing?"

[4–5] The Satan answered YHWH and said:
"Skin for skin![42] For all a man has he will give for his life.
However, send forth your hand[43] and affect his bone and his flesh!
I swear he will 'bless' (curse) you to your face!"

[6] YHWH said to the Satan:
"Here is he in your hand.
Only keep him in life."

[7] The Satan took leave of YHWH; and he[44] struck Job with a
    terrible inflammation,[45] from the sole of his foot to the top of
    his head.

---

42. A gnomic proverb. In light of the following clause one trades a skin only for
another skin. "Skin" can connote life (see Job 19:20); accordingly, one will respond to a
life threat only when one's own life is threatened. Alternatively one may interpret: "Skin
behind skin!"—Job's afflictions affected only his outer skin, his children and possessions;
if his own person, the skin below, so to speak, were affected, he would break down.
43. "Sending forth the hand" may connote bodily harm, even homicide; see for
example Esther 2:22.
44. Syntactically, the subject could be YHWH as well as the Satan; the ambiguity
reinforces the understanding that YHWH stands behind all Job's afflictions.
45. A skin disease, often rendered "boils," the sixth plague brought by YHWH upon
the Egyptians in Exodus 9:8–12. The root suggests heat.

9

[8] He took a potsherd with which to scratch himself as he sits in the ash-heap.

[9] Then his wife said to him:
"You are still holding-fast to your wholesomeness?!
'Bless' (curse) Elohim and die!"

[10] He said to her:
"You speak the speech of unseemly women!
Can we accept the good from Elohim and not accept the bad?"

In spite of all this, Job did not commit-a-sin with his lips.

[11] Job's three friends heard of all this evil that had overcome him;
so each man came from his place—
Eliphaz the Teimanite and Bildad the Shuhite and Zophar the Na'amathite[46]—
and they met at an appointed place to come to shake-the-head-in-pity and to console him.

[12] They lifted their eyes from afar and could not recognize him;
so they lifted their voices and they wept.

---

46. The names of Job's friends are derived from names of Edomites in Genesis 36. Eliphaz the Teimanite: see verse 11; Bildad the Shuhite: from Bedad and Husham (reversed) in verse 35; Zophar the Na'amathite: from Zepho and Timna (reversed) in verses 11–12. The name Job is equated with Jobab in verses 32–33, as it is in the ancient Greek translation and other ancient Jewish literature. For Teiman as a site in Edom (and not Yemen), see Jeremiah 49:7.

Each man tore his coat,
and they hurled dirt over their heads toward the sky.[47]

[13] They sat down on the ground with him for seven days and
    seven nights,
and no one speaks a word to him,
for they saw that his pain had grown very great.

---

47. The unusual phrase alludes to the production of the plague of inflammation by
Moses (Exodus 9:10). Since Job is suffering from "terrible inflammation," the friends' acts
of mourning symbolically show solidarity with him.

JOB'S OPENING DISCOURSE
(3:1–26; 4:12–21)

Job invokes a curse on the day of his birth and the night of his conception—after the fact; and if he had to have been born, he wishes he had been born dead. Reversing the conventional, Job seeks death and darkness rather than life and light. In the ancient Near East in general women would recite incantations for ease of childbirth and the health of the newborn. Job employs a similar genre for an opposite purpose. Job reproaches the deity for exposing people to a life of suffering and remaining indifferent to their fate.

[**3:1–2**] After that Job opened up his mouth and cursed his day (of birth).
Up spoke Job and he said:

[3] Let the day disappear, the day I was born,[1]

---

1. "Day" is repeated in translation for reasons of prosody.

And the night that announced: A man's been conceived![2]

[4] As for that day—Let it be darkness![3]
May he not summon it, Eloah from on high;
May nothing luminous shine on it!

[5] Let darkness, dead-darkness, expunge it [4]
Let hovering clouds engulf it!
Let daytime eclipses[5] obscure it!

[6] As for that night—Let pitch-dark remove it!
May it have no part[6] in the days of the year,
May it have no place in the count of the months!

[7] Yes, as for that night—Let it be sterile![7]
May no joy (of love) take place on it!

[8] May they condemn it—the cursers of Yamm,[8]

---

2. By referring to himself as "man" (*geber*) Job identifies himself with the "man" in verse 23 below; also note 10. The term also designates a pious sufferer; see Lamentations 3:1 and Psalm 88:5; and compare Psalm 94:12.

3. A parody of "Let there be light!" (Genesis 1:3).

4. For *gaal* "to disqualify," see Ezra 2:62 (= Nehemiah 7:64; so for example M. Kimhi).

5. *Kamrir* means "darkening"; compare *nikmar* "charred" (see for example M. Kimhi).

6. Reading *yehad*, literally, "to be at one with," with some traditional as well as modern commentators; for the same pair—*ba* and *yehad*—in parallelism, see Genesis 49:6.

7. The word for "sterile" also denotes, as in Arabic, a solitary crag (so Gordis, *Book of Job*). The image of the lone pillar reinforces our perception of Job's sense of isolation.

8. The mythological sea monster that God had to restrain in creating the earth (for example Psalm 74:13–14; see further Job 38:8–11). Although the Hebrew word is vocalized *yom*, the word for "day," the juxtaposition with Leviathan makes the primary reference clear. *Yom* is the Phoenician pronunciation of Yamm.

Those armed with a curse[9] for Leviathan!

[9] May the stars of the twilight turn dark,
That (the night) wait for the light—but there be none!
Let it see not a glimmer of dawn!

[10–12] For it would not lock the doors of my womb,[10]
And hide life's travails from my eyes.
Why couldn't I die after leaving the womb—
Just go out the loins and stop breathing?[11]
For what did knees have to receive me?[12]
For what were the breasts that I sucked?

[13–15] I could just have lain down in silence,
Slept and enjoyed my repose;
Together with kings and with counselors,
Who build palace-tombs[13] for themselves.
Or with nobles, possessors of gold,
Who fill up their grave-homes with silver.

---

9. The verb *'arar*, cognate to Arabic *'arra* "to vilify," is known in Hebrew in the form *'ariri* "disgraced" (see especially Jeremiah 22:30).

10. Job sees his mother's womb as his own; see the introduction to this volume. In contrast to Jeremiah, who curses the day of his birth but mentions his father, his mother, and the messenger who brought the good news (20:14–18), Job will not refer to any person involved in his birth. He even refers to himself at birth as a "man" (verse 3), not a child.

11. Compare Ecclesiastes 4:3.

12. Probably the knees of the mother (Genesis 30:3), possibly those of the father or grandfather (see Genesis 48:12; 50:23). Job refers to disembodied limbs and not to the people to whom they belong.

13. Literally, "ruins"; but for *ḥorabot* one may read *ḥaramot* "pyramids" (*mr* in Egyptian; *harama* in Arabic).

[16] Why couldn't I be like a stillborn,
Just covered over (in the sand),
Like babies who never saw light?

[17–19] There (in the grave)—no more restless are the troubled;[14]
And there the failing of strength find repose.
All prisoners are (there) at peace;
They hear not the voice of their oppressor.
The small and the great, there are the same;
And a slave is set free from his master.

[20–22] Why give light to one in travail?
Or life to those bitter of spirit?—
Those waiting for death, but there is none,
Though they dig for it more than for treasure![15]
Those singing for joy at the mouth of the tomb,[16]
Who are glad to be reaching the grave.

[23] (Why give light) to a man
Whose path is hidden from Eloah,[17]
Who screens him[18] off from his[19] sight?

[24] For my moans come to me like my bread,
And my growls are doled out like my water.

---

14. For this sense of *rasha*, ordinarily "wicked"—which is inapt here—see 34:29 (Ibn Ezra).

15. "Buried, covered over" treasure, echoing the "covered over" stillborn of verse 16 above.

16. Literally, at the stone "rolled across" the mouth of the tomb (compare *golel* in the Mishnah).

17. Drawing on Isaiah 40:27.

18. The man.

19. God's.

[25] A fear I have feared—and it's come about;
Just what I dreaded befell me.

[26] I've had no rest, I've had no quiet,
I've had no repose—restlessness comes.

*For many reasons the passage 4:12–21 should be read here, right after chap-
ter 3, as the conclusion of Job's opening speech. One may suppose that two
pages of ancient papyrus or parchment containing the two equal halves of
chapter 4 were accidentally interchanged in the course of the text's transmission. In an oft-compared Babylonian composition about a pious sufferer ("I
Shall Praise the Lord of Wisdom") it is the complainant, not the would-be
sage, who experiences a divine revelation. It is also Job the sufferer, not his
companions, who receives a theophany near the end of the book. More important, in the ensuing chapters both Eliphaz and Job refer to Job's claim to
have enjoyed a revelation. Further, Eliphaz (in chapter 15) and Bildad (in
chapter 25) cite the words of the revelation as Job's, and Elihu, who engages
only with the arguments of Job, quotes from it (33:15). These and other reasons for rearranging the two halves of chapter 4 will be indicated in the notes
(see also Ken Brown). The renegade spirit that discloses divine secrets to Job
recalls the Mesopotamian god Ea, who reveals the secret of the forthcoming
deluge to the human flood hero (Weinfeld).*

[**4:12–14**] Yet to me did a word come in stealth,
And my ear grasped a hint of it;[20]

---

20. Job spells out the apprehension to which he alluded in 3:25; compare 4:14, which
resumes 3:25.

In shudders from visions in the night,[21]
When slumber falls upon people.
Fear overcame me, and trembling;
As shivers set my bones to shaking.[22]

[15–16] For a spirit[23] passed across my face;
It set the hair of my flesh on end.
It stood still, but I could not discern its demeanor,[24]
(Nor) the form in front of my eyes.

A moaning and voice[25] did I hear:

[17–19] "Can a mortal be righteous before Eloah?[26]
Can a man be pure before his Maker?
If in his servants he puts no trust,
And in his angels he finds fault,[27]
Then all the more[28] those who dwell in clay houses,[29]

---

21. In 7:13–14 Job will blame God for giving him nightmares.

22. For *rob* "shivers" compare Akkadian *rūbu* and see Job 33:19 and 4:3 (with a slight revocalization). For the expression "bones shaking"—reading *hirhip* for *hiphid*—see Jeremiah 23:9 (Ginsberg, "Job the Patient"). In Hebrew script of all periods, *d* and *r* look alike.

23. An "angel" from the divine assembly, described in Job 1:6; 2:1; and elsewhere; see further 15:8.

24. Compare Job's language in 9:11 to his language here and in verse 15 above.

25. "A moaning and a voice" echoes the phrase often rendered "still (small) voice" in the revelation to Elijah (1 Kings 19:12).

26. The preposition *min* can also be understood as "more than," but so ironic a sense does not comport with the present context. For the usage of *min* found here, see Psalm 18:22, where the sense "more than" is impossible.

27. A borrowing from Arabic (Weber).

28. The expression *'ap* is short for *'ap ki* (as in the parallel passage 15:16); for the formula, "If . . . , then all the more so . . . ," see Deuteronomy 31:27; Proverbs 11:31.

29. A metaphor for the body.

Whose foundation is in the dust.[30]

They are quashed before twilight;[31]
[20] From day-break till evening they are crushed;
When it is not even nightfall[32] they forever disappear.[33]

[21] Their tent-pin[34] is pulled up on them;[35]
They die without (ever finding) knowledge."[36]

---

30. Humans were created out of the dust of the earth; Genesis 2:7; see also Job 10:9; 32:6.

31. Compare Arabic 'asā "evening" (Ginsberg, "Job the Patient") and Hebrew 'ashash "grow dark" in Psalm 6:8.

32. The participle of *sim* with prefixed *mem* is a ghost-word in pre-Mishnaic Hebrew. Revocalize *mashayim,* comparing Arabic *masā'* "evening," Late Hebrew 'emesh "last evening."

33. This phrase together with "Let the day disappear" (3:3) frames Job's first discourse.

34. Reading *yetedam* for *yitram* "their tent-cord" on the basis of Isaiah 33:20 (Luzzatto and others). The letters *d* and *r* look alike.

35. Life is figured here as a tent one puts up and takes down.

36. For the idea, compare Proverbs 5:23; 10:22.

ELIPHAZ'S FIRST DISCOURSE
(4:1–11; 5:1–27)

Agitated by Job's unexpected outburst, Eliphaz reassures him that he will ultimately be restored to circumstances befitting the righteous—an estate and a
brood of children. Eliphaz deduces this from his perspective on the wicked: for
a time they may thrive, but in the end they suffer a sorry fate; the converse
must be true of the righteous. He explains Job's suffering not only as a tempo-
rary stage in the life of a human but also as a form of divine discipline—a
sign of God's concern, a warning to remain faithful, not a punishment. In the
course of his response, Eliphaz disparages Job's claim to have received a message from a member of the divine circle.

[4:1] Up spoke Eliphaz the Teimanite and he said:

[2] To hold back[1] a word from you—(even) you could not!

---

1. Vocalizing *hanasa* (for *nanissa*, "has someone tried?") and parsing *hanas* as an
older Aramaic form of Hebrew *'anas*, "to withhold, restrain"; see Esther 1:8; Daniel 4:6.

To refrain from words[2]—who could?[3]

[3–4] It is you who have fortified the trembling,[4]
And limp arms you have strengthened;
The stumbling would your words raise up,
And buckling knees would you stiffen.[5]

[5] But now that (calamity) has come to you, you cannot (bear it);
It touches you yourself, and you are shaken.

[6] Hasn't your reverence been your backbone,
And your integrity[6] your source-of-strength?[7]

[7] Think: what innocent ever disappeared?
And where have the upright been destroyed?

[8] Whenever I have seen plowers of suffering,[8]
And sowers of travail—it is they who reap it.

---

2. Using Aramaic *millin*, the equivalent of Hebrew *dabar* in the preceding line.

3. For *la'a* "cannot" and *yakol* "can" as antonyms, compare Exodus 7:18 and 21.

4. For *yisser* in the sense of "fortify," see Hosea 7:15. For *rabbim* "many" I read *rabim* "trembling"; see the note on 4:14 above and the introduction to this volume. These two unusual verbal usages produce a secondary meaning: "You have instructed many."

5. The language is drawn from Isaiah 35:3.

6. Literally, "the wholeness of your ways." See the comment on "whole (in heart)" at 1:1.

7. For this understanding of the syntax, see already the reading of Saadia Gaon and the Tosafist commentary to Babylonian Talmud *Baba Metzia* 58b.

8. The word-pair *'awen-'amal* can denote either "iniquity" or "suffering." Job uses *'amal* in 3:10 and 20 in the latter sense, and that is apparently Eliphaz's intention throughout his speech; see also Psalm 90:10 and probably Numbers 23:21. However, especially in view of the fact that a similar image is used of cultivating wrongdoing in Proverbs 11:18; 14:22; and 22:8, Job—and the reader—may be hearing in Eliphaz's words the implication that he has sinned, even though Eliphaz does not express that perception in his first discourse (compare Fullerton).

[9] By the breath of Eloah they disappear,
By the wind of his nostrils they come to an end.

[10–11] The lion[9] growls and the beast roars;
But the teeth of the predators (finally) crack.
The lion perishes[10] for lack of prey,
And the lion whelps are eradicated.

[5:1][11] Call out now! Does anyone answer you?
To whom of the holy ones can you turn?[12]

[2] For exasperation can kill the rogue.
And passion can bring death to the fool.

[3–4] I have myself seen a rogue striking roots,
And have observed the homestead of fools.[13]
His sons are kept far from relief;[14]
Oppressed at the city-gate,[15] no one delivers them.

---

9. Eliphaz's use of the lion metaphor may have been prompted by Job's use of "growls" in 3:24. The lion is a typical image of the wicked; see Psalms 7:3; 17:12; 22:14; and others. The poet employs five different terms for "lion" in this passage, a feat that cannot be duplicated in English.

10. The use of the same verb as in verse 9 links the lion and its fate to the wicked that it metaphorically represents.

11. 4:12–21 has been moved to precede 4:1; see above for the passage and for a brief justification of the move.

12. Eliphaz mocks what to him is Job's illusion that he has experienced a divine revelation.

13. Reading peta'im "fools" for pit'om "suddenly" (compare Proverbs 14:18) and finding behind wa'eqqob "I cursed" a synonym for "I have seen," possibly wa'abbit.

14. They are easily victimized in legal proceedings, which are held at the town gate. Compare Isaiah 59:11.

15. Compare Proverbs 22:22.

[5] As for his harvest—famine[16] will consume it;
And their substance[17]—desiccation[18] will remove it;
And drought[19] will devour[20] their wealth.

[6–7] For suffering does not stem from the dust,
Nor does travail grow from the ground.[21]
But a human is born to travail,[22]
As "sons of Resheph"[23] fly up high.

[8] Rather I would seek out El,
Before Elohim would I lodge my complaint.[24]

[9–10] (El) who performs great things too deep to probe,

---

16. Vocalizing *ra'ab* for *ra'eb* "the hungry." The verse is extraordinarily difficult, and no translations are convincing.

17. Reading *we'ulam* (see Psalm 73:4; so for example Tur-Sinai).

18. Reconstructing a noun from the root *ts-n-m* "dried out" (Genesis 41:23).

19. Reading *tsama'* "thirst, drought," often found in conjunction with *ra'ab* (Deuteronomy 28:48; Isaiah 5:13) for otherwise unknown *tsammim*.

20. Reading *sapa'* (compare Hebrew *mispo'* "fodder" and Ugaritic *sapa'a* "consume") for *sha'ap* "pant, aspire."

21. "Ground" (*'adama*) is of the same stem as "human" (*'adam*), which appears in the next verse.

22. Or through revocalizing: *yolid* "gives birth (to travail)"; compare Job 15:34–35; Psalm 7:15.

23. Arrows. Resheph is a Canaanite god of pestilence and is sometimes depicted with arrows, symbolizing his afflictions; he is called Lord of the Arrow. Compare Psalm 76:4; see 6:4 for an echo by Job. Others interpret "sons of flame, sparks," comparing Song of Songs 8:6.

24. Eliphaz resumes the thought of verse 1. He lays heavy emphasis on "El" (the name of God throughout Canaan, meaning "God") through sound repetition: *'ulam* ("rather") ... *'el 'el* ("to El") ... *(we)'el 'elohim* ("and to Elohim"). The phrase "lodge a complaint," literally, "place a word," is an apparent calque from Babylonian, where it carries the connotation of lodging a legal complaint (Paul). Eliphaz may not intend to suggest that Job sue God, but Job, as it turns out, would seem to infer the idea.

Wondrous things, beyond number;[25]
Who gives rain over the face of the earth,
And sends water over the face of the ranges.

[11–13] Placing the lowly up high,
So the stooped[26] attain relief.
Who thwarts the plans of the treacherous,
So their hands can perform nothing clever.
Who catches the wise in their treachery,
So the perverse take their counsel in haste.

[14] In daytime they encounter darkness,
It's like night when they grope at midday.[27]

[15] He has saved the swordless from the tormentor,[28]
And the needy from the powerful.

[16] Thus is there hope for the poor;
As (all) injustice is silenced.[29]

[17–18] Happy is the mortal whom Eloah reproves—
Do not reject Shaddai's discipline.[30]

---

25. Eliphaz draws on clichés; compare for example Amos 4:13; 5:8; Psalms 136:4; 145:3.
26. In Biblical Hebrew *qoded* "stooped, lowly, depressed" seems to merge with *qoder* "dark, depressed" (Psalms 35:14; 38:7; 42:10; 43:2).
27. Compare Job 12:25; Deuteronomy 28:29.
28. Reading *mippi ham* (compare Job 36:16: *mippi sar* "from adversity") for *mippihem* "from them."
29. Literally, "and injustice shuts its mouth."
30. Shaddai is another name for the deity; see the Note on (No:) Translating the Names of God. Eliphaz explains Job's afflictions as only a warning from God, to keep him

For once he inflicts pain, he binds up;
Once he strikes, his own hands heal.[31]

[19] From six misfortunes he will deliver you,
In seven no harm will affect you.[32]

[20–23] In famine he will ransom you from Death,[33]
And in war, from the sword.
From the lashing of a slanderous-tongue you'll be hidden;
And from oncoming disaster you will have no fear.
At a demon and at stones (at your feet)[34] you will laugh;
And from wild animals[35] you will have no fear.
You'll be rather in league with the stones of the field,
And the beasts of the field will be at peace with you.[36]

[24] You will find[37] your abode is at peace;
You'll take stock of your homestead with nothing amiss.

---

honest, as it were. For this conventional wisdom, compare Deuteronomy 8:5; Psalm 94:12; Proverbs 3:11–12.

31. Compare Deuteronomy 32:39; Hosea 6:1.

32. For the nuance of "affect," see on 1:11. In numerical sequences of x, then x+1, in the Bible, it is the latter number that is definitive. Seven misfortunes will be enumerated.

33. Perhaps an allusion to the Canaanite god of death, Mot; compare 18:13–14.

34. Both *shod* "disaster" and *kapan*, Aramaic for "famine," have already been enumerated. Accordingly, revocalize them as *shed* "demon" and *kepin*, Aramaic for "stones"; see *kepim* in Job 30:6. "Stones" is recapitulated (in Hebrew) in the next verse. Compare Psalm 91 for the combined dangers of demons and stones that may cause one to stumble or bruise (verses 6, 12–13).

35. Literally, "the animals of the earth."

36. Compare Hosea 2:20.

37. Literally, "know."

[25–26] You will find[38] that your seed is numerous,
And your offshoots like the grass of the earth.
You will reach the grave like a ripened-stalk,[39]
Like the rising of grain in its season.

[27] You see, we have probed this—it's true.
Pray listen, and know it yourself!

---

38. Literally, "know."

39. Compare *qelah* in Rabbinic Hebrew and see Proverbs 11:30, where instead of *l-q-h* read *q-l-h* "stalk" (of life-breath) in parallelism with "tree of life."

JOB'S RESPONSE TO ELIPHAZ
(6:1–7:21)

Job rejects Eliphaz's counsel and rebuts his main arguments. Job does not believe he is receiving mere divine discipline—his afflictions are sapping his life! Nor can he believe he will live to see a bright future—he has neither the endurance nor the time; the lifespan is simply not that long, and his, he believes, is nearing its end. Job's real complaint is with the deity, and so, in parallel with his verbal sparring with his companions, he turns to God, reiterating his desire to die (6:8–9). Eliphaz had ridiculed Job's claim to have experienced a revelation from the divine circle. Job defiantly replies that his one consolation is that he disclosed and did not suppress the spirit's unsettling message (6:10). In his description of his friends' betrayal, Job evokes Jeremiah's complaint against his perceived abandonment by God (Jeremiah 15:18).

[**6:**1] Up spoke Job and he said:

[2–3] Were my anguish weighed, yes, weighed,
And my vexation borne with it on scales,
It would be heavier than the sand at the sea.

That is why my speech is a garble (to you).[1]

[4] Shaddai's arrows are in me,[2]
and my life-spirit drinks up their venom.[3]
Eloah's terrors are arrayed against me.

[5] Does a wild ass bray (when it's) in the meadow?
Does an ox low (when it's) at its feed?[4]

[6–7] Can the insipid be eaten without salt?
Is there any taste in the juice of chubeza?[5]
My gullet refuses to touch it;
To me it's like sickening food.

[8–9] Would someone grant what I ask?
Would Eloah grant what I hope for?
That Eloah would comply and crush me!
Release his hand and cleave me!

[10] Yet would I have this one consolation,
When I'd writhe and recoil as he'd show no mercy:

---

1. "Garble" renders a unique noun derived from "stammer" (Obadiah 1:16).

2. There is early Canaanite (Ugaritic) evidence to the effect that Shaddai was a god of the field (Hebrew *sadeh*) who hunts, making the association with arrows very apt. Here he is depicted like the Canaanite god Resheph; see 5:7 with the comment there.

3. Because both "life-spirit" and "venom" are feminine, like the verb, a reverse of subject and object is plausible: "Their venom saps my life-spirit."

4. I only speak out because I am in anguish.

5. A Middle Eastern herb, lacking in taste. The Hebrew word (read *halamit*) is known from ancient Syria (Alalakh). The term for "taste" is polysemous, denoting "reason" as well; see also 12:11 and 34:3. Job is telling Eliphaz that his argument is lacking in reason and that he will have none of it.

That I did not conceal the words of the holy one.[6]

[11–12] What strength have I that I should wait?
What span (of life) that I should show patience?
Is my strength the strength of stone?[7]
Is my flesh made of bronze?[8]

[13] Alas,[9] there is no more power in me;
And my wits are driven out of me.

[14] Why is one who turns from evil put to shame?[10]
And one who fears Shaddai accursed?[11]

[15–17] My brothers have betrayed me like a wadi,
Like the bed that the wadis stream through.
They turn dark from ice,
And snow piles up[12] on them.
In the season they are scorched, they are devastated;
In the seasonal heat, they dissolve from their place.[13]

[18–20] Caravans turn a twisting route,

---

6. Not the deity but the spirit that appeared in 4:12–21; "holy ones" in Job refers to the angels (see 5:1; 15:15).

7. Like Leviathan (41:16).

8. Like Behemoth (40:18).

9. For ha'im in this sense, see Numbers 17:28.

10. Reading lama sar me-ra' yehussad (Ginsberg, "Studies") for the impossible traditional text. For the verb, compare Proverbs 25:10 (hissed "shames").

11. Reading ye'uzzar for ya'azor "he helps"; compare Akkadian ezēru and Phoenician 'zr. Note how Job unwittingly evokes his characterization by the narrator and the deity in 1:1, 8; 2:3.

12. Taking yit'alem as a pseudo-Aramaized form of yit'arem.

13. Compare Job 24:19.

They go into the desert and are lost.
Caravans from Tema look out (for the wadis),
Convoys from Sheba hold out for them.
They balk for having relied (on them).
They arrive at (the spot) and are dismayed.

[21] Thus have you now become naught (to me);[14]
You see a terrifying sight, and you are seized with fear.

[22–23] Have I ever asked you, "Give of yours for me"?
Or "From your means pay out for me"?
Or "Rescue me from an assailant"?
Or "Ransom me from brigands"?

[24] Enlighten me and I'll silence myself;
Just inform me where I've done (you) wrong!

[25–26] Why do my honest[15] words provoke (you)?
Why do they prompt you to reproach?
Do you regard (my) words as mere wind?[16]
This desperate man's speech as mere wind?

[27] Would you cast lots[17] even over an orphan?
Would you barter even over your friend?

---

14. Job's language echoes that of Eliphaz in 4:5, suggesting that here, as elsewhere in the discourse, Job is responding to Eliphaz.

15. "Straight" in speech. The term "straight (of path)" (see 1:1) is used of the "heart," the seat of speech, in 33:3.

16. A different Old Greek reading shows the traditional text was unclear. For *ha-le-hokah* "as reproach," I read *ha-le-ruah*.

17. Compare Psalm 22:19. The lots are cast to determine who benefits.

[28] So now please oblige and face me;
I swear I won't lie to your faces.[18]

[29–30] Turn back now—there will be no corruption!
Turn back—I hold to what's right!
Is there corruption on my tongue?
Does my palate not discern false speech?[19]

Job responds to Eliphaz's argument that if Job would only be patient he would find that his lot would return to its former goodness (God wounds, then heals; 5:18). Job addresses not only his companions; he begins to confront God. Attention from the deity is what the righteous typically desire. Job now regards divine attention as malevolent.

[7:1] Does a mortal not serve a fixed sentence on earth,[20]
His days like a hired-hand's days?

[2–3] Like a slave panting for some shade,
Or a hired-hand waiting for his earnings,
So am I meted out moons[21] of futility;
Nights of suffering are allotted to me.

---

18. The verb "to lie" alludes to the wadi that has run dry of verses 15–20; the term for "wadi" in the verse being parodied, Jeremiah 15:18, is of the same root, "to disappoint." Job's connotation is: I would not fail you the way you have failed me.

19. See Psalm 5:10, where *hawwa* is in parallel with "no truthfulness."

20. Compare Isaiah 40:2.

21. In parallel with "nights," we should understand "moons" literally (so Tur-Sinai)—a metonym for the night—rather than as "months," as it is customarily understood. Job has not been suffering all that long a time.

[4] When I lie down I think: When can I rise?
Every evening![22]
I am sated with tossing till dawn.

[5] My flesh is cloaked with worms and lumps of dirt;
My skin is welted[23] and decays.

[6] My days run faster than the shuttle in a loom,
Running out for lack of cord, lack of hope.[24]

[7] Keep in mind that my life is mere wind;
My eye will no more see the good.

[8] O eye of my Observer, you will see me no longer!
Your eyes are upon me—and I'm gone.

[9–10] A cloud dissipates and passes;
So does one gone down to Sheol[25] never come up again.
He does not return to his home;
His place knows him not anymore.[26]

[11] And so I will not hold back my mouth!
I will speak out of tightness of breath,[27]

---

22. Reading *middei* for *middad,* which would mean "tossing." If the received text is correct, then we would seem to have an ancient explanatory gloss on the text: "Tossing at evening."
23. Many derive from Ethiopic, "to congeal" and therefore "to scab," but context suggests cracking of the skin (so for example Malbim).
24. Hebrew *tiqwa* means both "cord" and "hope."
25. The netherworld.
26. The same line is used in Psalm 103:16 in describing the ephemeral nature of life.
27. Distress. "Breath" is the same word as "wind" in verse 7 above.

Complain out of bitterness of spirit.

[12] Am I Yamm?[28]
Or am I Tannin?[29]
Then why[30] do you place me under guard?

[13–14] When I think: My bed will give me comfort,
My couch will relieve my complaint,
You terrify me with nightmares,
You torment me with visions.

[15] My throat[31] would rather choke,
(Choosing) death over pain.[32]

[16] I'm fed up! I won't live forever!
Stop (tormenting) me! For my days are mere breath.[33]

[17–18] What is a mortal that you treat him as important?[34]
Why do you pay him any mind,
Take account of him each morning,
Test him every minute?

---

28. See the comment on 3:10 above. The symbol of the watery chaos is the arch enemy of God.

29. A primeval sea serpent, a form of Yamm.

30. Not "that" but interrogative; see Jeremiah 8:22 (where *maddua'* "why?" glosses the more archaic use of *ki*, cognate to *'eka* in Ugaritic).

31. "Throat" is the same word as "spirit" in verse 11 above.

32. Reading *'atsbotai* (see 9:28 and Psalm 147:3) for *'atsmotai* "my bones."

33. The same term used by Qohelet (Ecclesiastes) when he says, "All is mere breath!" (1:2 etc.).

34. These two verses are a parody of Psalm 8:5–6 (so for example Fishbane):
"What is a mortal, that you pay him mind, / or a human that you take account of him?
"You have made him but a little less than God; / you have crowned him with honor and glory."

[19] Why can't you just look away from me,
Let go for just a swallow of spit?[35]

[20] If I've sinned, what can I do to you,
O Watcher of Humankind?
Why have you made me your target?[36]
How could I be a burden to you?[37]

[21] Why can't you pardon my transgression,[38]
Commute my punishment?
For I'll soon be lying in the dirt—
And when you seek me, I'll be gone.

---

35. For the instant it takes to swallow one's spit.

36. See 6:4.

37. The Hebrew was corrected by an ancient scribe to the euphemism "to myself," but the original reading is acknowledged in rabbinic literature.

38. The verb "to pardon" is literally "to lift (the transgression from off the perpetrator)," thereby producing a play on "burden" (what is carried, the same verb as "to lift"): Job asks the deity, who should have no difficulty in bearing him, to lift off his burden—his presumed sin.

BILDAD'S FIRST DISCOURSE
(8:1–22)

Bildad, like Eliphaz, still trusts in Job's innocence. Accordingly, he overlooks most of the disasters that befall Job's estate and the wretched skin disease that plagues his person; and he deigns to justify the most horrific tragedy in terms of divine retribution: Job's children were put down by the deity because they (must have) sinned, probably blaspheming the name of God (they sinned against El—verse 4)—as Job had himself imagined they might have done (see 1:5). Otherwise, the deity would be unjust, a claim implied by Job but regarded as impossible by Bildad. Like Eliphaz, Bildad invokes traditional wisdom and, in support of the doctrine of just retribution, invokes images that depict the disintegration of the wicked and the thriving of the righteous. Straying from the particulars of Job's situation, Bildad cites a cliché to the effect that Job, if he remains righteous, will be happy while his enemies are dismayed.

[**8:**1] Up spoke Bildad the Shuhite and he said:

[2] How long will you make such declarations?

(How long) will the words of your mouth be a massive wind?[1]

[3] Would El corrupt what is just?
Would Shaddai corrupt what is right?

[4] If your sons committed a sin against him,
He has dispatched them for their offense.[2]

[5–7] If you would only seek El,[3]
Seek compassion from Shaddai,
If you are pure and straight (of ways),
Then will he protect you,[4]
And make your rightful homestead whole.[5]
Though your former days were meager,
Your latter days will exceedingly thrive.

[8–9] Just inquire of the former generations,
And consider[6] the deep-wisdom[7] of our ancestors;[8]
For we are only yesterday and have no knowledge;
For our days on earth are but a (fleeting) shadow.

---

1. Bildad confirms Job's accusation of his companions in 6:26.
2. For *shillaḥ* as delivering to death, see 14:20; compare Jeremiah 15:1.
3. The verb "seek" echoes Job's address of the deity in 7:21.
4. The use of the rare verb "protect" alludes to the deity's protection of Israel like a bird hovering over its nest (Deuteronomy 32:11).
5. Bildad is nearly parroting Eliphaz in 5:24. The term for "whole" here is the same as that rendered "at peace" there.
6. Reading *bonen* for *konen* ("establish") with the Syriac translation and others.
7. Cognate to the verb "to probe" in 5:27.
8. The traditional text reads "their ancestors"; the final *mem* is a ligature of what should be *nun* and *waw*—a well-known scribal phenomenon (Weiss, "Ligature"). A clearer instance occurs at 15:18.

[10] They will surely instruct you, they'll tell you;
Out of their hearts they will utter words:[9]

[11–12] "Can papyrus grow without marshland?
Can a canebrake thrive without water?[10]
While yet in the flower, it cannot be plucked;
And it withers even sooner than grass."

[13] Thus is the fate[11] of all who reject El;
The hope of the blasphemer vanishes.

[14–15] His stronghold is gossamer,[12]
And his trust a spider's house.
When he leans on his house, it will not stand up;
He will hold onto it, but it will not stand firm.

Bildad now describes the righteous.[13]

[16–17] He remains moist even in the sun;
And out of his spring his sapling grows.
His roots intertwine round a pile-of-stones,

---

9. For the heart (mind) as the seat of speech, see for example Psalm 19:15; 49:4; Proverbs 24:2; and especially Ecclesiastes 5:1, where we have a locution similar to the one used here. Bildad's quotation of apparently proverbial expressions mimics Job in 6:5–6.

10. The terms for "papyrus plant" and "meadow" are Egyptian loanwords.

11. Reading *'aharit* for *'orhot* ("the paths of"). The parallel to "hope" is "fate," not "paths"; see Jeremiah 29:11; Proverbs 23:18; 24:14.

12. The meaning "gossamer" was discerned already by Saadia Gaon. The word *yaqut* is an apparent borrowing from Akkadian *qe ettuti* "spider's web."

13. The righteous is introduced without an antecedent, leading some commentators to assume that a verse has been accidentally omitted. However, the rhetoric is consistent: images of the wicked were presented without introduction as well. The riddle of the image will be solved in verse 20, as the image of the wicked was explained in verse 13.

He can cut through even a house of stones.[14]

[18–19] If he is transplanted from his place,
So that it denies him: "I don't recognize you,"
Then he moves his growth-path,[15]
And sprouts from another (piece of) ground [16]

[20] For El will never reject the whole (of heart);
He will never lend support to evildoers.

[21–22] Yet[17] will your mouth fill with laughter,
And your lips with jubilation.[18]
Your adversaries are clad in defeat;
And the abode of the wicked—is no more!

---

14. A bed of rocks. The verb *haza*, ordinarily "to see," is a pseudo-Aramaism for Hebrew *hatsa* "cleave in two."

15. For *mesos* ("joy of"), which does not make sense here, read *yamish* or possibly (without changing a letter) *moshesh* "he moves (it)," which would be a unique form.

16. The *waw* at the end of *yitsmahu* is superfluous.

17. The adverb *'ad* is the Aramaic equivalent of Hebrew *'od*, used already at 1:18.

18. The proper use of the mouth, lectures Bildad, is smiling in satisfaction, not raising questions about divine justice (verses 2–3). Compare Psalm 126:2.

JOB'S RESPONSE TO BILDAD
(9:1–10:22)

The burden of Bildad's argument is to convince Job that God upholds the principle of just retribution: those who had sinned (Job's children) were punished (by death), and the righteous (in the present case, Job) is alive. This doctrine, proclaims Bildad, has been transmitted from generation to generation. Job responds to the arguments for divine justice made by Bildad, and by Eliphaz before him, by challenging the very notion that God is essentially just. Basing himself on the revelation of the rogue spirit in 4:17–21, Job submits that the deity finds humanity unworthy and therefore deserving of (unjust) punishment (9:2). God refuses to consider a human challenge, intimidating any challengers into acquiescence with his destructive power. In a typical parody of biblical piety, Job takes traditional images and vocabulary in praise of the deity's creative prowess and presents them in a negative light. He imagines that were it not for God's intimidation, he would take God to court and sue for justice. But alas, there is no magistrate who could prevail on the deity to play fair; to the contrary, God would falsely incriminate Job in order to beat him at trial.

[**9:**1] Up spoke Job and he said:

[2] I in fact know this is true:
"How can a mortal be righteous before God?"[1]

[3] If one wanted to press charges against him,
Not once in a thousand would he respond.

[4] The wise of heart and stern of strength[2]—
Who has ever coerced him[3] and come out whole?

[5–6] Him who moves mountains without their knowing;
Who overturns them in his anger.
Who shakes the land from its place,
So that its pillars tremble.[4]

[7–9] Who commands the sun so it does not shine;
Who seals the celestial lights.
Who spreads out the sky all alone;[5]
And who steps on the back of Sea.[6]
Who has made the Hyades, Orion,
The Pleiades and the South-Wind Chanters.[7]

---

1. A paraphrase of the spirit in 4:17.

2. Using this phrase, which ordinarily denotes subtle ornness, in reference to the deity is parodic; see Deuteronomy 2:30.

3. See Deuteronomy 2:30, where the deity "hardens the spirit" (will) of Israel's opponent.

4. The earth was imagined as resting on pillars; for example Psalm 75:4.

5. Borrowed from Isaiah 44:24, where God's being the sole creator is more to the point.

6. Stepping on the back of an enemy is a gesture of triumph; see Deuteronomy 33:29. Sea is both the Canaanite deity Yamm (see Job 7:12) and the sea.

7. These are all constellations. In the light of classical mythology, the constellations are, like Sea (Yamm), resistant powers that had to be subdued at the time of creation.

[10] Who performs great things too deep to probe,
And wondrous things, beyond number.[8]

[11] Since he can cross without my seeing him,
Pass by without my discerning him,

[12] He can snatch—and who can restrain him?
Who will say to him: "What are you doing?"

[13] (Since) Eloah will not restrain his anger—
Even the soldiers of Rahab[9] cower beneath him—

[14] How could I call him to account,
Choose my charges[10] against him?

[15–16] Even in the right, I would get no response;
Even if I implored my opponent in court.
But if I would summon and he would respond,
I do not trust he would hear my complaint.[11]

[17–18] He would push me on the hair-line,[12]
And multiply my wounds for no cause.[13]

---

8. A parody of Eliphaz in 5:9.

9. A biblical name for the primeval sea monster, like Sea / Yamm and Leviathan (Psalm 89:10–11).

10. The term "word(s)" often denotes legal matters.

11. Literally, "he would give ear to my voice."

12. A gesture indicating the rejection of a legal claim, attested in Alalakh (north Syria) in the seventeenth century BCE (Wiseman, 38). Others understand "hair" (as in 4:15) as its homonym "storm," but in Job that word is always spelled with *samekh* not *sin*.

13. "For nothing" in Job 1:9. Job does not realize how right he is.

He would not let me return breath,[14]
For he saturates me with poison.[15]

[19] If it's a matter of strength, then he is the strong;
And if a legal proceeding, who can convene us?[16]

[20] Even were I in the right, his mouth[17] would condemn me.
(Even) were I innocent,[18] he would wrong me.[19]

[21] I am innocent—I care[20] not for my self;
I'm fed up with my life.[21]

[22] It is all the same.
And so I declare:
The innocent and the guilty he brings to (the same) end.[22]

[23] While (his) scourge brings death to fools,[23]
He laughs at the trials of the spotless.

---

14. That is, make any statement; compare 15:13. There may be a secondary sense of not allowing Job even to "restore his breath" (compare Psalm 23:3).

15. Reading *bimrorim* (Lamentations 3:15). Compare the image in Job 6:4.

16. Reading final—*nu* "us" for—*ni* "me."

17. Read *piw* for *pi* "my mouth." The virtually synonymous parallel line makes this certain. That Job incriminates himself is Eliphaz's later contention (15:5–6), not Job's. An ancient scribe surely sanitized the reading here; but the point is elaborated by Job in verses 30–31 below.

18. "Whole (of heart)" in Job 1:1, 3.

19. Reading *ya'ashqeni* (with metathesis).

20. For this sense of *yada'*, see for example Exodus 2:25; Psalm 1:6.

21. Compare 7:16.

22. This radical claim finds a parallel in Ecclesiastes (7:15; 4:14). It is exceeded only by Ezekiel 21:8, where the deity himself threatens to annihilate both the righteous and the wicked.

23. Reading *peta'im* for *pit'om* "suddenly," as I did in 5:3; compare the ancient Greek translation.

[24] The earth is handed over to the wicked;[24]
He covers the eyes of its judges.[25]
If it is not he, then who?

[25–26] Meanwhile my days go faster than a runner;[26]
They flee having seen nothing good.
They pass on like boats made of reeds,
Like an eagle swooping down on food.[27]

[27–28] Were I to say, "I'll ignore my complaint,
I'll forgo my sullen face[28] and be happy,"
I'd dread all my afflictions;
I know you will not find me spotless.

[29] I will be found guilty.
So why should I strive in vain?[29]

[30–31] Were I to wash myself with soap-plant,[30]
And cleanse my palms with lye,[31]

---

24. Job overturns the conventional wisdom according to which the reverent "inherit the earth" (for example Psalm 25:13; 37:9).

25. So that they cannot render justice.

26. A racing messenger; see for example 2 Samuel 18:19–32. Job returns to the theme of 7:6.

27. Compare the images in Habakkuk 1:8.

28. For "face" alone in the sense of a sullen mien, see for example 1 Samuel 1:18.

29. The term for "in vain" is *hebel* "mere breath" (as in Qohelet 1:2).

30. Reading with the traditional *Ketib* (written form) rather than the Masoretic reading "with snow water," which is a much less apt parallel.

31. The word *bor*, employed instead of conventional *borit*, usually means "pit" and therefore produces a pun with the term for pit in the following couplet. The verse parodies Jeremiah 2:22, where God says to the people of Judah: "Even if you clean (yourself) with soap and apply a lot of lye, your sin will be a stain in my sight." Job boldly accuses the deity of falsely incriminating him.

You would plunge me into the pit,[32]
So even my clothing would abhor me.

[32] For he is not like me a man I could call to account;[33]
(With whom) we could join in a lawsuit.

[33–35] If only[34] were between us a prosecutor,
Who would lay his hand on us both;
Who would remove his[35] rod from upon me,
So his awe would not terrify me,
Then could I speak and not fear him—
For I am not being right toward myself.[36]

*Job begins to overcome his intimidation and to build a case against the deity.
Assuming that he is being held accountable for minor misdeeds (see 7:16ff.),
Job makes a classic argument, found already in second millennium BCE Hittite prayers from Asia Minor: If I am sinful, it is your fault for having made
me this way. You should be more tolerant of your creature's infractions. Returning to earlier themes (his opening discourse), Job asks why he had to be
born at all and why he should be so closely watched, when he will soon be
gone. Job does not yet sue God formally; but he lays out a hypothetical case.*

[**10:1**] My entire being despises my life.

---

32. "Pit" also connotes the grave (for example 33:18).
33. Compare the usage in verse 14 above.
34. Reading *lu'* for *lo'* with some ancient translations and many commentators. For *lu'*
spelled with *a'eph*, see 2 Samuel 19:7; compare also 1 Samuel 14:30; Isaiah 48:18; 63:19.
35. The deity's.
36. For the force of the expression "not right," see 2 Kings 17:9.

I would prepare a complaint on my behalf,
I would speak in the bitterness of my being;

[2] I would say to Eloah: "Do not condemn me!
Let me know of what you accuse me![37]

[3] Does it do you any good to do wrong?
To reject the effort of your hands?
While you shine favor on the schemes of the wicked?

[4–5] Have you eyes that are of flesh?
Do you see as a mortal sees?
Are your days like the days of a mortal?
Are your years like those of a man?

[6–7] When you go looking for my crime,
And investigate my sin,
You know very well I am not guilty—
But no one can rescue from your hand![38]

[8–9] Your hands formed me[39] and made me,
Put me together[40]—then destroyed me!
Mind now, it is you who made me like clay,
And will return me to the dust!

[10–11] Have you not poured me out like milk,

---

37. Job assumes that the deity holds him guilty of some transgressions.
38. Job typically converts a positive statement of God's power from Deuteronomy 32:39 ("no one can rescue from my hand") to a negative one.
39. The verb in context also connotes "pain" (see 9:28), from the same root.
40. Literally, "together and about."

And jelled me like cheese?
Clothed me in skin and flesh,
And woven me in bones and sinews?

[12] You have handled me with life and devotion,
And your providence has protected my spirit.

[13–14] But certain things you've kept hidden in your heart;
I know this is what you think:[41]
If I commit a sin, you'll be watching me;
You'll not declare me clean of my crime.

[15] If I am guilty—then woe be to me!
But even in the right, I could not hold up my head.
Be sated with (my) disgrace,
And regard my affliction![42]

[16–17] And if (my head) were to loom, you would hunt me down
    like a lion;
You would work wonders[43] against me over and over!
You would renew your hostilities[44] toward me,
As your anger grows great against me,
Arraying reinforcements against me.[45]

---

41. Literally, "with you."

42. Or "being sated with disgrace, and experiencing affliction." Compare the expression "to see (experience) affliction," known from Lamentations 3:1 (and compare "we have seen evil/disaster" in Psalm 90:15). Job here inverts the conventional perspective by addressing the deity.

43. As in wreaking plagues (see Deuteronomy 28:59); compare *pela'im* "appalling acts" in Lamentation 1:9.

44. Compare Arabic *'adawa*.

45. More literally, "replacements and army are with me."

45

[18–19] So why did you take me out of the womb?
Would I had died, with no eye seeing me!
Would I had been as though I had not been;
Would I had been carried from womb to tomb.

[20–22] Very few are the days of my lifespan[46]—
Look away[47] from me, so I may have a respite.
Before I go and do not return,
To a land of darkness and deep-shade;
A land whose brightness is like pitch-black,
Deep-shade and disorder;
That shines like pitch-black."[48]

---

46. For the written form (*Ketib*) *yḥdl*, which is read *wḥdl* in the Masoretic tradition, read *ḥeldi* "my lifespan," which is found in parallelism with "my days" in Psalm 39:6; compare the ancient Greek and Syriac translations.

47. Reading *she'eh* for *yashit*, "he puts," which does not suit the context. Job uses the same phrase in 7:19; and for the combination of *sha'ah* (*Hiph'il*) and *hiblig* "have a respite," compare Psalm 39:14.

48. The realm of the dead is depicted, as in chapter 3, as the reverse of the land of the living—a gloomy abode where daylight is darkness. So already Saadia Gaon; and see Ginsberg, "Unrecognized Allusion."

ZOPHAR'S FIRST DISCOURSE
(11:1–20)

Neither Eliphaz nor Bildad has accused Job of transgression, but their insistence on the deity's perfect justice has reinforced Job's sense that they perceive him to be in the wrong. Zophar believes that since Job seems afflicted, he must be suffering punishment at the hands of a just God. However, he is willing to give Job's integrity the benefit of the doubt: Zophar makes the original suggestion that Job has been made by God to forget his transgression (verse 6). Only the deity knows Job's sin, and Zophar wishes the deity would set the record straight by revealing it to Job. Job has wanted the same thing. But since divine secrets are inaccessible to humans, all Job can do, according to Zophar, is appeal to God in penitence and thereby be rehabilitated. In underscoring the unknowability of the divine, Zophar anticipates Elihu (chapters 32–37 with 28).

[**11:1**] Up spoke Zophar the Na'amathite and he said:

[2–3] Should one long of speech be unanswered?

Should a man keen of lips be found in the right?[1]
Yet people keep silent before you;
You blather,[2] but no one refutes[3] you.

[4] You say, "My doctrine is pure;
I have been clean[4] in your[5] eyes."

[5–6] But if only Eloah would speak,
And open his lips with you,
And reveal to you unseen secrets of wisdom—
For there are two sides to sage knowledge[6]—
You should know Eloah is making you forget your sin!

[7–9] Can you fathom the depths of Eloah?
Can you reach the limit of Shaddai?
The heights of heaven—can you get there?[7]
Deeper than Sheol[8]—can you know it?[9]

---

1. Should a person be allowed to win an argument just because he is adept in speaking?

2. Reading *wa-te'alleg* from *leshon 'ilgim* "twisted language" (Isaiah 32:4) for *wa-til'ag* "you mock." Or, the use of *la'ag* is ironic, as it is used (as a metathesized form of *'lg*) in the sense of "stammer, blather" in Isaiah 28:11. Zophar is punning on Job's use of *la'ag* "mock, laugh," said by him of the deity in 9:23.

3. For this usage, compare Proverbs 25:8.

4. Echoing *bor* "lye" in 9:30.

5. God's.

6. Some wisdom is accessible, but some is esoteric and known only to God (Nahmanides).

7. Literally, "can you do, achieve?"

8. The netherworld, the realm of the dead.

9. "Know" has the nuance of direct contact. This couplet is a variant of an age-old line of Mesopotamian wisdom: "The tallest man cannot reach the sky; the broadest man cannot encompass the earth" (Greenspahn).

It[10] is longer than the earth in measure,[11]
And wider than the sea.

[10] If he were to snatch,[12] or to deliver,[13]
Or to corral[14]—who can restrain him?

[11] He alone knows when people are false;
He sees evil and recognizes deceit.[15]

[12] But a hollow man will be filled with heart,[16]
When a wild ass[17] is born to a human.[18]

[13–15] If you set aright your heart,
And raise your palms in prayer,[19]
If you put evil far from your hand,
That no corruption reside in your tents

---

10. Divine wisdom (verse 6).

11. The Hebrew syntax is a peculiarity of the Joban poet; compare 15:10: "Greater than your father in days."

12. Reading *yahtop* for *yahlop* "he passes by," which is unsuitable in this context. Zophar is responding to Job's assertion about God in 9:12.

13. The verb can suggest surrendering someone to an enemy (for example Lamentations 2:7) or quarantining someone in a house (for example Leviticus 13:5).

14. Gather a person up—a unique usage.

15. In light of the parallelism to *shaw'* and *'awen* "nought, falsity" and "evil, iniquity," respectively, it seems most apt to take the deceptive-looking negative particle *lo'* here as a substantive, as in 6:21.

16. That is, a mind, intelligence.

17. There are two consecutive terms for "ass"; one is apparently an explanatory scribal gloss on the other.

18. The verse is notoriously difficult; I follow the sensible and linguistically sound interpretation of Good.

19. Literally, "your palms toward Him," toward God.

Then will your estate be bare of blemish;[20]
You will be rock solid, and you will not fear.[21]

[16] For you will have forgotten your travails,
Remembering them only as water that's flowed.

[17] (Your) lifespan will rise (brighter) than noon;
Like the gleam of morning will you be.[22]

[18–19] You will feel safe for there is hope;
You will burrow in and lie down in safety.
You will repose[23] with no cause to tremble;
Many will seek your guidance, (as before).[24]

[20] But the eyes of the wicked will grow dim;[25]
Their refuge will disappear,
And their hope is—chagrin![26]

---

20. The received text has: "Then will you raise your face without blemish." However, in view of Zophar's reference to Job's habitation, literally, "tents," in the preceding line, the intention seems to be something like what both Eliphaz and Bildad had assured Job at the end of their speeches: that he will enjoy a restored life and a rebuilt household (see especially 5:24). Accordingly, I divide the words slightly differently and read a few of the letters slightly differently: *tishpeh naweka mi-mum*, literally, "your estate will be bare (pristine), without blemish." For *nishpeh* describing a bare (unforested) hill, see Isaiah 13:2. For *naweh* as a feminine noun, see for example 8:6. Zophar would seem to blame the destruction of Job's estate on his having committed some trespass thereon.

21. A response to Job's expression of fear in 9:34–35 and elsewhere.

22. The language echoes Job in 10:20–22.

23. The image is of a recumbent animal.

24. Literally, "Many will entreat your face." Compare Job's role as described by Eliphaz in 4:3–4 and by Job himself in 29:7–25.

25. An expression of unfulfilled expectations; compare Psalm 69:4.

26. Compare the expression "to cause chagrin" in Job 31:38–39. The poet is partial to the oxymoron; compare for example "shines like pitch-black" in 10:22.

JOB'S RESPONSE TO ZOPHAR
(12:1–14:22)

*Job has heard each of his three companions rehearse the traditional wisdom—
that one who trusts in and turns to the deity will ultimately thrive. Job begins
this lengthy reply by demonstrating that he, too, is well versed in conventional
lore. Satirizing the tradition (see especially the parody of Deuteronomy 32:7b
in verses 7–8), Job regales his friends with a series of mock proverbs and wise
sayings, several of them closely parodying known biblical passages, to the effect that the pious can rest secure and that the deity governs both nature and
human affairs.*

[**12:**1] Up spoke Job and he said:

[2–3] Truly you are people-of-intelligence [1]
And with you wisdom will die.
I have a heart[2] just like you.

---

1. There is likely a play on the Egyptian word for intelligence *'am*, which is a regular
Hebrew term for "people" (suggested to me by Stephen Geller).
2. A mind; an apparent response to Zophar in 11:12.

I fall no lower than you.[3]
And who doesn't have such (sayings) as these?:

[4–6] "One who laughs at calamity and disaster,[4]
Calls out to Eloah and is answered—
The laugh of the wholly righteous—
He shows contempt for catastrophe,[5]
At a time of devastation[6] is at ease.
He is firm when the foot might stumble.[7]
Tents[8] are tranquil at a time of marauders,[9]
Secure at a time of those who rile El—
At whatever the hand of Eloah has wrought."

[7–8] Rather, ask the behemoth[10]—and it will instruct you.[11]
Or the fowl of the sky—and it will tell you.

---

3. I am not inferior to you.

4. This verse begins a series of platitudes, reminiscent of those of his companions. It is clear from the next line that a third-person subject is called for. For *sehoq* read *soheq* in conformity with the participle that follows in the next line. For *le-re'ehu* I read *le-ra'ah* and for *'ehyeh* I read *howah* "disaster" (see Isaiah 47:11). (I am indebted to Ginsberg for most of the reconstruction of this passage.)

5. Read *le-pid*; for *pid* "catastrophe," see Job 30:24 and 31:29 as well as Proverbs 24:22.

6. For the notoriously difficult *le'ashtut* I read *le'et sheyt*, "at the time of devastation"; for *shet* (written with *aleph*), see Lamentations 3:47 and compare the cognate *sho'ah* in Proverbs 3:25. For the spelling without *aleph*, compare the spelling of *se'et* "grandeur" without *aleph* in Job 41:17 and of *re'em* "wild ox" without *aleph* in Job 39:10. The resulting sense recalls the advice of Proverbs 1:33b.

7. Compare Proverbs 25:19; for the phrase and the construction of the preceding line, compare Deuteronomy 32:35.

8. Of the righteous.

9. "At a time of" is mentally supplied from the preceding lines.

10. A quasi-mythological beast, similar to the hippopotamus; see Job 40:14–24.

11. A parody of Deuteronomy 32:7, and more immediately Bildad (8:8–10), in which the teaching of the elders is recommended.

Or converse with the earth[12]—and it will instruct you;
And the fish of the sea will recount to you.

[9] Who does not know all these things—
"That the hand of YHWH has done this?"[13]

[10] "In whose hand is the breath of all life,
The spirit of all human flesh.

[11] You see, an ear examines words,
As a palate tastes food:[14]

[12] In the elderly is wisdom,
And length of days is intelligence.[15]

[13] With him[16] are wisdom and might.
His are good counsel and intelligence.

[14] He can destroy so it cannot be rebuilt;
He can close a man in so it can't be reopened.[17]

---

12. The animals of the earth are likely meant.

13. Job is making a direct quotation of Isaiah 41:20: "so that they will see and know and observe and learn that the hand of YHWH has done this, that the Holy One of Israel has created it'—otherwise Job would not be using the personal name of the Israelite God (see the introduction to this volume). The present passage seems to draw many images and expressions from Isaiah 41–45.

14. "Taste" also connotes reasoning; see 6:6. From here through verse 24 is another string of mock wisdom sayings.

15. Compare Eliphaz in 15:9–10.

16. God. There is no immediate antecedent because the sayings are excerpted from their sources.

17. Job turns Eliphaz's traditional saying of 5:18 into a negative.

[15] He can hold back the water so that (things) dry up;
Then he can release them so they convulse the earth.[18]

[16] With him are power and sage knowledge;
His are the mistaken and the misleader.[19]

[17–19] He causes counselors to go barefoot,[20]
And judges he turns mad.
The girdles[21] of kings he loosens,
And removes[22] the strap on their loins.[23]
He causes priests to go barefoot,
And the stalwarts he leads to ruin.[24]

[20–21] He removes language from orators,[25]
And takes sense away from elders.
He heaps contempt on leaders,[26]
As the belt of (their) armor[27] he slackens.

---

18. Job parodies Eliphaz's beneficent image of divine rain-giving in 5:10; see also Isaiah 41:18; 42:15; 44:3, 27.

19. Literally, "the one who causes others to be mistaken." A very negative type, who trips up the blind (Deuteronomy 27:18) and corrupts the upright (Proverbs 28:10). Job may be parodying what Eliphaz says of God's outsmarting the wise in 5:14–15.

20. A sign of desolation; see Micah 1:8 and compare Isaiah 20:2.

21. Reading *mosar* (see Job 39:5; Jeremiah 2:2; Psalm 107:14) for *musar* "discipline, instruction."

22. Reading *wayyasar* for *wayye'sor* "and he girds," which conveys the contrary sense. Compare Isaiah 45:1. Ironically "remove" puns on "gird."

23. Those doing combat would gird their loins; see Job 38:3; 40:7.

24. For a similar usage of the verb, see Proverbs 21:12.

25. Reading *na'manim* for *ne'emanim* "the faithful"; compare Jeremiah 23:31.

26. Compare Psalm 107:40a.

27. See Job 41:7.

[22] He uncovers the depths of darkness,
And brings deep-shade into light.[28]

[23] He elevates nations, then disperses them;[29]
He expands nations, then deports them.[30]

[24–25] He removes the heart[31] from the landed folk's chiefs,[32]
Making them stray in a trackless waste.[33]
They grope in darkness without light,[34]
As he makes them stray like a drunkard."[35]

*Having demonstrated his familiarity with traditional wisdom, Job sums up,
berates his companions for their insensitivity, and lays out his legal challenge
to the deity—a challenge he had considered no more than a whimsy in chapter 9. Job now realizes he has nothing to lose by calling God to account, and
he implores his companions to show no partiality as they listen to his case.*

[**13:1–2**] You see, my eye has seen it all;
My ear has heard and taken notice.

---

28. Compare Job 28:3, 11. Job would seem to be parodying Zophar in chapter 11.

29. More precisely, leading them into exile or oblivion.

30. The verb *hinhah* nearly always connotes a supportive guidance. Here Job appears
to be using it ironically—leading away into exile. Others, basing themselves on some of
the ancient translations, read *wayyanihem* "he leaves them aside, abandons them."

31. Mind, courage.

32. Literally, "heads."

33. Identical to Psalm 107:40; compare Isaiah 42:16.

34. Compare Deuteronomy 28:29.

35. Compare Isaiah 19:14, where it is said of Egypt.

What you know, I know as well;
I fall no lower than you.[36]

[3] Rather I would speak to Shaddai;
It is an argument with El I desire.[37]

[4] But you, rather, are smearers of lies,[38]
False physicians, all of you!

[5-6] If only you would keep silent, yes, silent—
For that would be wisdom for you!
Pray hear my argued case;
And pay heed to my lips' accusations.

[7-8] Will you speak corruptly to El?
To him will you speak with guile?
Will you show favor to his face?[39]
Or will you argue[40] on his behalf?

[9-11] Would it be well were he to interrogate you?
Will you (try to) delude him as you would a mortal?
He would reprove,[41] yes, reprove you,
Were you to secretly favor his face.
Wouldn't his majesty terrify you?

---

36. A reprise of 12:3.
37. Job ironically responds to Eliphaz's challenge in 5:8.
38. The Hebrew *topel* is polysemous: a smearer of slander, a smearer of ointment.
39. Literally, "lift up his face." Favoritism in a judicial proceeding is forbidden; see Exodus 23:3, 6. So is lying; see Exodus 23:7.
40. Here "argue" is the same term as "accus(ation)" in verse 6.
41. The same term as "argue" in verses 3 and 6; for the sense of "reprove," see 5:17.

And wouldn't his fear fall upon you?

[12] Your pronouncements[42] are like maxims[43] of dust;[44]
Your responses[45]—like lumps of clay.

[13] Keep silent before me, so that I may speak—
Whatever may come upon me!

[14–15] I will take my flesh[46] in my teeth,
And I will place my life-breath in my hand.
Though he slay me, I will no longer wait[47]—
I will accuse him of his ways to his face![48]

[16] Only he can be my salvation;[49]
For he would allow no blasphemer to approach.

[17] Hear, yes, hear my words—

---

42. Compare Akkadian *zakāru* and Arabic *dhakara* "to say"; and Hebrew *zeker* in the sense of "name" (for example Exodus 3:15; compare Job 18:17).

43. The form "maxims" is polysemous, also indicating "resemblance"; the latter meaning is suggested by the preposition *le-*("to") in the following line.

44. More precisely "ash," but in biblical parlance "ash" is often combined with "dust"; see for example Job 30:19.

45. Compare Arabic *jawab* "reply." There is a pun on *gab* ᶜ *ump*."

46. That is, my self. The first two words of the verse are a mistaken repetition (dittography) from the end of the preceding verse (according to many scholars).

47. The ancient rabbis (for example Mishna Sota 5:5) and Masoretic scribes want to read "I will wait for him," reading *lo* for *lo'*, but the whole point of this passage is that Job is pressing his case. I therefore read with the traditional spelling (*Ketib*), supported by Elihu's rebuttal in 35:14.

48. Reading "his ways" for the Masoretic Text's "my ways," which makes no sense and results from an ancient pious correction, intended to protect God's honor. See Job 21:31.

49. There is a touch of irony in this admission; the phrase is modeled on such pious expressions as Exodus 15:2 and Isaiah 12:2.

My declaration—with your ears.

[18–19] Here: I am laying out my lawsuit.
I know I am in the right.
Who would argue the case with me?
I would then keep silent—and expire.

[20–21] Only two things you must not do to me—
Then will I not hide from your face:
Put your hand far from upon me,
And terrify me not with your awesome mien!

[22] Either you summon, and I will respond;
Or I will speak, and you will answer me.

[23] How many are my crimes and my sins?
My transgression and my sin—tell me what they are!

[24] Why do you hide your face,
And reckon me your enemy?[50]

[25–26] Would you scare off a driven leaf?[51]
Or[52] put to flight dry tumbleweed?
Then why do you issue me a poisonous writ?[53]

---

50. "Enemy" ('oyeb) puns on Job's name ('iyyob); compare 7:12; 19:11.
51. An ironic reversal of the curse in Leviticus 26:36, where the "driven leaf" puts the offenders to flight.
52. Reading we'im for we'et "and"; we have here a triple question formula, the same as in 7:12.
53. For merorot as "poison," and not simply "bitterness," see 20:14; compare Deuteronomy 32:32. The writing Job refers to is the bill of indictment he imagines stands behind the deity's harsh affliction of him; see 31:35.

And take me to task[54] for the crimes of my youth?[55]

[27] And mark my feet with lime,[56]
And watch my every step,
And follow[57] the tracks of my feet?[58]

The divine hostility that Job perceives is being directed at him does not make sense in the light of humanity's insignificance. Job goes on to describe a person's insubstantiality, contrasting a tree, which can regenerate, with a human, who cannot. Ironically, a human perishes like an inanimate rock, which crumbles (verses 18–19). Job asks for a period of respite—to be placed temporarily among the dead—reprising the middle part of his first discourse. The completion of Job's last speech in this cycle recalls phrases, images, and arguments from his preceding discourses.

[14:1–2] A human, born of woman,
Is short of days and sated with restlessness.
He sprouts like a flower and withers.
He flees[59] like a shadow and does not stay.

---

54. The traditional text's *wa-torisheni*, usually understood as "handing down an inheritance, imparting," has the opposite meaning in Biblical Hebrew. I read (with Ginsberg) *wa-tirsheni*, from Aramaic *resha* "to hold accountable take action against someone."

55. Compare Psalm 25:7.

56. Reading *be-sid* for *ba-sad* "in stocks," which makes no sense: fettered feet cannot go anywhere, so they cannot be followed; compare M. Kimhi. Job develops the same point in 14:16.

57. More literally: "You make imprints in the roots of (that is, the tracks left by) my feet."

58. Verse 28 does not make sense here; it apparently follows 14:1–2, from which it was accidentally misplaced.

59. "Flees" (*yibrah*) punningly suggests in this context the verb "blossoms" (*yiprah*).

[**13**:28] He wears away like a waterskin,[60]
Like a garment eaten by a moth.[61]

[**14**:3] Even on such a one would you train your eyes,[62]
Bringing me[63] into lawcourt with you?

[4] Who can produce pure out of tainted?
No one can![64]

[5] When his days are curtailed,[65]
The number of his months in your hands.[66]
You have set him limits he cannot overrun.[67]

[6] Look away from him and let him stop (being tormented)![68]
Until like a hired-hand he fulfills[69] his day.

[7–9] For there is hope[70] for a tree:

---

60. Reading *ke-roqeb,* from Aramaic, for *ke-raqab* "like rot." The reading is supported by some ancient versions, and compare the use of the verb "wear away" with the Hebrew term for "waterskins" (*no'dot*) in Joshua 9:13. The verse clearly belongs here, as an illustration of 14:1.

61. Compare Isaiah 50:9.

62. Compare Jeremiah 32:19. "Such a one" connotes "me"; see Psalm 34:7.

63. Many prefer to read "him" (*'oto*) for "me" (*'oti*) with some of the ancient translations; but it is typical of Job to meld his particular case with his general observations.

64. Compare the message of the spirit in 4:17–21. "Pure" and "tainted" are ritual categories, like edible and inedible animals (see Leviticus 11), implying that even the deity cannot transform one into the other.

65. Compare Isaiah 10:23; for the general sense see Psalm 90:9–10.

66. Literally, "with you."

67. An echo of Jeremiah 5:22, alluding to God's mythological restraint of the sea; compare Job 7:12.

68. An echo of Job 7:16 and 19.

69. Compare the usage in Leviticus 26:34. An echo of Job 7:2.

70. Contrast Job 7:6 and compare 11:18.

If it is cut, it can go on to replace itself,
And its shoot[71] will not stop (growing).
Even if its root grows old in the ground,
And its stump goes dead in the earth,
At the mere scent of water it will flower,
And like a sapling produce a plant![72]

[10] But a man—he dies and grows feeble;[73]
A human expires—and where is he?[74]

[11] Water can run out of the sea;[75]
And a river can drain and dry out.[76]

[12] So does a man lie down never to arise;
Until the sky is no more, they will not awaken,
They will not be aroused from their sleep.[77]

[13] Would that you conceal me in Sheol!
Hide me away till your anger subsides!
Set me a period—and then call me to mind![78]

---

71. "Sapling" in Job 8:16. Job counters Bildad's image of the flourishing righteous.

72. The Hebrew is replete with ironies: "sapling" here is literally "(newly) planted," and the term rendered here "plant" is "harvested (produce)"—literally, "the cut."

73. The verbs seem to be in reverse order; but the verb "grow feeble" (*wa-yehelash*) plays ironically on "replace itself" (*yahalip*) in verse 3.

74. Echoes Job 7:8, 21 (said of Job); 8:18, 22 (said of the wicked).

75. The sea can run out of water.

76. "Drain and dry out" (*yeherab we-yabesh*) echoes "grow feeble" in verse 10.

77. Contrast Isaiah 26:19 and Daniel 12:2, according to which the dead can be resurrected from the sleep of death.

78. Job seeks a reprieve from his life of affliction—a "(fixed) period" of time to lie among the dead; compare Job's idealization of death in 3:13–24.

[14] If a man dies, can he revive?
All the days of my fixed sentence[79] I will wait[80]—
Until my replacement arrives.[81]

[15] Summon and I will answer you—
When you long for the work of your hands![82]

[16–17] Perhaps now when you count my steps[83]
You will not keep my sins in mind.
Seal[84] my transgression in a pouch,[85]
And plaster over my crime!

[18–19] And yet,[86] a cliff will fall and crumble;
A mountain will be moved from its place;[87]
Rocks are worn down by water;
A torrent sweeps away the earth's dust;
So do you obliterate a mortal's hope.

[20] You assault him continually—and he passes on;
You disfigure him—and then you dispatch him.

---

79. Of life on earth; see 7:1.

80. An echo of 13:15.

81. See verse 7 above. Job will be happy to "live" in the realm of the dead for a period, until he is regrettably relieved by someone else.

82. Sarcastic: when you miss me and need to restore me to my miserable life. Compare 10:8–13.

83. See 13:27.

84. In parallel with the verb in the following clause, this verb should be read not as vocalized—as a passive participle (*hatum*)—but as an imperative: *hatom*.

85. If the evidence against Job is kept in a pouch—as was the ancient practice preceding a trial—Job cannot be convicted. For the image, compare Hosea 13:12 (Holtz).

86. Job ceases to fantasize and offers his own image of human disintegration.

87. An echo of Job 9:5.

[21] If his sons receive honor—he does not know;
And if they are diminished—he does not see them.

[22] But his family[88] is pained over him;
And his household[89] mourns him.[90]

---

88. Literally, "flesh"; see Genesis 37:27.
89. Literally, "his self"; see Genesis 12:5.
90. A more literal interpretation is: "Only his flesh pains him; and his life-force dries up on him." The image of a family's mourning is familiar from the Babylonian poem of the pious sufferer "Let Me Praise the Lord of Wisdom" and other ancient texts.

ELIPHAZ'S SECOND DISCOURSE
(15:1–35]

Opening the second cycle of dialogue, Eliphaz reacts to Job's stubborn conten-
tion that he is in the right and the deity in the wrong. First, he berates Job for
claiming to have received a divine revelation, parodying Job's report of the
spirit's message in 4:17–19 in verses 14–16. (The failure of almost all inter-
preters to recognize this leads to their missing the point of the discourse and
to the widespread mistranslation of several verses, contrary to the normal
meanings of the words.) Then Eliphaz counters Job's denial of just retribution
by citing ostensibly traditional sayings, enumerating the misfortunes attend-
ing the wicked. Both arguments of Eliphaz extend statements he had made in
the first round (5:1 and 8; and 4:8–11, respectively). Eliphaz may be under-
stood benevolently to be warning Job to repent before it is too late.

[**15:**1] Up spoke Eliphaz the Teimanite, and he said:

[2–3] Does a sage[1] utter such windy speech,

---

1. In the preceding discourse (especially chapters 12 and 14), Job had sought to
demonstrate his familiarity with wisdom sayings and images.

And fill his belly with an east wind,
Arguing a case to no advantage,
With words that bring no benefit?

[4] You go so far as to abrogate piety,
And expropriate talk from the presence of El.[2]

[5–6] For your own mouth denounces your crime,
As you adopt a devious tongue.
Your own mouth condemns you, not I;
Your own lips testify against you.[3]

[7] Are you the first human to have been born?
Were you engendered before the hills?[4]

[8] Have you been listening in the divine council,
Expropriating wisdom to yourself?

[9–10] What do you know that we do not know,
That you understand—but not intelligible to us?[5]

---

2. That is, the divine council. Only prophets can participate in the heavenly council (see Jeremiah 23:22). The plain meaning of this verse, missed by virtually all preceding translators, is evident from verse 8 below. Job claimed to have heard the report from a member of the divine council in 4:12–21. The fact that that passage is misplaced in the book (see there) is clear from what Eliphaz says in this chapter. Eavesdropping on conversations in heaven is regarded as a severe offense; compare the Qur'an 37:35, where those listening in on divine dialogue are destined for meteor and comet attacks.

3. Your admission of listening in on divine conversation demonstrates your transgressive inclination. Eliphaz counters Job's claim that God's mouth indicts him unjustly (see 9:20).

4. Only someone present at the creation could have direct knowledge of God and God's ways; see Proverbs 8:22–31, verse 25 of which is quoted here by Eliphaz.

5. Literally, "not with us"—a pun on "people-of-intelligence" in 12:2. Eliphaz counters Job's claims in 12:3 and 13:1–2.

With us are the gray-haired and aged—
Greater in years than your father.

[11] Are the consolations of these (men)[6] too few for you—
That you (claim to) have[7] a secret word?[8]

[12–13] How your heart carries you away,
And how haughty are your eyes,[9]
That you answer El with your wind,[10]
And out of your mouth put forth such words:[11]

[14–16] "What is a mortal that he be rendered-pure?
That a man born of a woman[12] be found-right?
If he[13] puts no trust in his holy ones,[14]
And the heavens[15] are not pure in his eyes,
All the more one detested and depraved,[16]
Who drinks corruption as though it were water!"[17]

---

6. For the short form of "these" (not "El"—who is not known to have comforted Job!), see for example Genesis 19:25; 26:3 (Gersonides).

7. "Have"—literally, "is with you"—a play on "is not with (intelligible to) us" in verse 10 above.

8. An allusion to 4:12.

9. Reading *yerumun* "are elevated"; see Proverbs 6:17; 30:13 (Luzzatto).

10. Compare verse 2 above. It is a formulaic reference to speech; see 35:4.

11. A clear introduction to direct discourse; see 8:10 and the preface to this speech. Eliphaz is mocking Job.

12. Echoing Job in 14:1; compare 25:4.

13. The reference to the deity without a nearby antecedent demonstrates that the passage is based on 4:17–19, where the mention of God is explicit.

14. The angels; see 5:1 and the comment there.

15. A metonym for the angels; see Job 25:5.

16. Compare Psalm 14:1–3. Eliphaz's characterization of humanity pushes Job's satirically; Job had only said (in the name of the spirit) that humans were flawed and mortal, not altogether decadent.

17. Compare the image in 34:7.

[17–18] I will declare to you—listen to me!
What I have seen[18]—I'll recount to you.
What the sages have revealed
And did not conceal from our ancestors:[19]

[19] "To them alone[20] was the land given,[21]
And no alien has passed among them.[22]

[20–21] The wicked all his days is caught up in a tempest,[23]
And the years in store for the terrible are few.
The sound of the frightful is ever in his ears,
Even in peace-time, the marauder overtakes him.[24]

[22–23] He'll not again feel secure[25] in the dark,
And he's destined for the sword.
He's ordained to be food for the vulture,[26]
He knows a dark day is set firm for him.

---

18. Eliphaz's reference to "seeing" is no more than a cliché of traditional wisdom; compare 4:8.

19. Reading 'aboteinu for the traditional text's nonsensical 'abotam "their ancestors." The letters nw were written close together and misread as final mem; compare at 8:8.

20. To the righteous, the antithesis of the wicked. The antecedent of "them" is missing because Eliphaz is quoting an excerpt from a known context.

21. Contra Job's contention that "the land has been given to the hand of the wicked" (9:24).

22. And profaned the land; see Joel 4:17.

23. Literally, "he whirls." An allusion to Jeremiah 23:19, the only other place this unusual verb form occurs, in which a "whirling storm" is said to befall the wicked.

24. An echo of Job's quoted wisdom in 12:6.

25. The same expression as "puts no trust" in verse 15 above.

26. Reading no'ad for noded "wandering"; and 'ayyah for 'ayyeh "where?" with support of the Old Greek translation.

[24] Hostility terrifies him[27] and distress attacks him,
Like a king fitted out for the fray."

[25–27] Because he bent his arm toward El,[28]
And played the warrior against Shaddai,[29]
Would run against him with strong neck,[30]
With his thickly plated armor—
Because he has covered his face with fat,[31]
And put blubber[32] over his sinews,

[28] Now he must dwell in ruined towns,
In uninhabitable houses,
Fated to be mounds.

[29] He will not be rich,[33]
His substance will not last,
And his wealth will not grow.[34]

---

27. Reading the verb as written as a singular, and joining the following verb to the noun that precedes it. The second verb echoes Job's usage in 14:20.

28. Eliphaz turns from platitudes to an elaboration of the last image.

29. Taking a divine prerogative; see Isaiah 42:13. There is a subtle allusion to Job's having characterized himself at the outset as a "man" (*geber*), cognate to "warrior" (*gibbor*).

30. A figure for arrogance; compare the phrase "strong neck" in Psalm 75:6.

31. That is, acted rebelliously; see Deuteronomy 32 15.

32. An Arabic borrowing.

33. It is possible that Eliphaz resumes his quotation of traditional wisdom, which reminds one of Bildad's citation of conventional imagery in chapter 8. Verse 35 below is a virtual quotation of Psalm 7:15.

34. Literally, "their wealth will not extend over the land." The term for "wealth" is borrowed from Babylonian *nēmelu* with metathesis.

[30] He cannot move out of the dark.[35]
Fierce heat dries up his shoot,[36]
He's removed by the wind of his mouth.[37]

[31] Let him not trust in salvation,[38]
For it will prove false.[39]

[32–33] His palm tree[40] will wither[41] before its time,
And his foliage will not thrive.
He sheds his unripened fruit like a grapevine,
Casts off his blossoms like an olive tree.

[34] For the impudent's company is sterile and lone,[42]
As fire consumes the tents of graft.

[35] They conceive travail and give birth to suffering;[43]
Their own bellies[44] generate deceit.

---

35. The next clause makes clear that the image is of the wicked as a hapless plant; see 8:11–15.

36. An echo of Job's use of the term in 14:7.

37. See 4:9. The reference to the deity is implicit by dint of the allusion.

38. Reading the sequence *b-sh-w n-t-'-h* as a single word, partly corrupted: *b'tshu'ah.* For the idiom, see Psalms 78:22; 146:3.

39. Compare Psalms 60:13 and 108:12 for the phrase "and false is human salvation."

40. Attaching the last word of the preceding verse and reading *timorato* "his palm tree" (see 1 Kings 6:29, 32, 35, with support from the ancient Greek translation) for *temurato* "his recompense."

41. Reading *timmal* "it will wither"; see 18:16 and compare Abraham ibn Ezra's commentary.

42. See 3:7 with the note.

43. An echo of 5:7 and a virtual quotation of Isaiah 59:4 and especially Psalm 7:15.

44. Connoting "womb, bowels," as in 3:10–11 and elsewhere.

JOB'S RESPONSE TO ELIPHAZ
(16:1–17:16)

Job begins to show empathy for the friends' position. As he goes on to explain, someone like Job, who is afflicted by the deity, is stigmatized and thought to deserve derision. Job realizes that his physical deterioration appears to people as evidence that he deserves his suffering. God has made Job the object of his depredations and of other people's scorn. Ironically to Job, God is the witness to his innocence—but he remains aloof, high in the heavens (compare 3:23 and further 21:22; 22:12–14). Job weaves back and forth among his points, alternating between appeals to his companions for understanding and to the deity for vindication. Returning to the motif of 7:6 and elsewhere, he ends on a note of hopelessness.

[**16:1**] Up spoke Job and he said:

[2–3] I have heard many such (sayings)—

Futile[1] comforters are you all:
"Is there no end to windy speech?"[2]
Or "What provokes you to speak this way?"[3]

[4–5] Even I would speak like you,
If you were in my place;
I would harangue[4] you with words,
And shake my head at you.[5]
I would embolden you with my mouth,
And spare[6] you my consolations![7]

[6] If I speak out, my pain will not be spared.
But if I desist, how will it leave me?

[7] By now he has worn me down;
You[8] have devastated my entire company.[9]

---

1. The term *'amal* more often denotes "travail, suffering" and thus connotes it here: the companions' efforts in consolation ironically produce even greater suffering for Job. For *'amal* as a poetic synonym of *shaw'* "naught" see Job 7:3.
2. A paraphrase of Eliphaz in 15:2. Job is (inexactly) quoting the kinds of things his companions have said.
3. Compare Job in 6:25–26.
4. An apparent influence from Babylonian *habā'u* in the sense of "to harangue" (Finkelstein).
5. An apotropaic gesture, to ward off evil; see Jeremiah 18:16; Lamentations 2:15.
6. Reading *'ahsop* for *yahsop* "he would spare."
7. Literally, "the movement of my lips," a gesture of condolence; see Job 2:11 and 42:11; elsewhere used of the head (Psalm 44:15).
8. Job resumes his complaints against the deity. The shift between third and second person (enallage) is unusual but not unique.
9. Job's family and friends. The term *'edah* in this context echoes Eliphaz in 15:34 but also puns on *'ed* "(hostile) witness" in the following verse. For the alienation of Job's family from him, see chapters 19 and 29 and compare Psalm 88:9.

[8] You have shriveled me, and this has become a stigma;[10]
My gauntness stands up and testifies against me.[11]

[9] As his anger rages,[12] he strikes a hostile pose;[13]
He gnashes his teeth at me;
My enemy sharpens his eyes at me.[14]

[10] People's[15] mouths gape at me,[16]
They strike my cheeks to shame me;[17]
They all form gangs against me.[18]

[11] It is El who delivers me to the depraved,
Who thrusts[19] me into the hands of the wicked.

[12] I was tranquil, then he tore me apart,
Seized me by the neck and ripped me apart.[20]

He set me up as his target.[21]

---

10. Literally, "a witness." Diminishing him with a terrible skin disease, the deity has created a witness to his being on the wrong side of God.

11. Alternatively: "You have subdued me and become (my) prosecutor; my repudiator has stood up and testified against me."

12. The idiomatic term for "raging" connotes the mauling of a wild animal. For the idiom, see Amos 1:11.

13. The verb *satam*, "to take a hostile attitude, act with malice," echoes the name of the Satan.

14. Suggests the evil eye; compare Psalm 35:19.

15. Literally, "their"—enemies roundabout, encouraged by the divine stigma.

16. Compare Psalm 22:14; Lamentations 2:16.

17. Compare Lamentations 3:30.

18. Compare Isaiah 31:4.

19. Literally, "makes me fall" (Numbers 22:32).

20. Recall Job's image of God as a lion on the prowl in 10:16.

21. Recall Job's image of God the hostile warrior in 7:21; compare Lamentations 3:12.

[13–14] His archers surround me;
He pierces my innards, showing no mercy;[22]
He spills my gall to the ground.
He opens against me breach upon breach;[23]
He runs at me like a warrior.[24]

[15] I sewed sackcloth onto my hide;
And sank my horn[25] into the dust.

[16] My face has turned sullen[26] from weeping;
Over my bright-eyes is deathly-dark—

[17] Over no wrongdoing by my hand;
And my prayer is pure:

[18] "O earth, do not cover my (innocent) blood![27]
Let my outrage have no place (to hide) "

[19] For even now my witness is in the heavens,
The one who knows the truth[28] is on high.

[20] My companions are my taunters;[29]
My eye pines for Eloah!

---

22. A refrain in Lamentations (2:2. 7, 21; 3:43).
23. God is said to breach Job's exterior the way an attacker breaches a city wall.
24. Echoing Eliphaz in 15:24.
25. A metaphor for pride; see Psalm 75:5–6. Job, the victimized stag, must lower his horns in defeat.
26. Literally, "darkened"; compare Lamentations 5 17.
27. Many find here an allusion to Genesis 4 10.
28. "Knows the truth" is literally "testifier," a synonym (in Aramaic) for "witness."
29. "Taunters" (see Psalm 119:51) differently derived means "advocates" (for example Job 33:23). Again ironically, Job's consolers are his disparagers (see 16:2 above).

[21] For this man[30] has a case with Eloah,
(Like) a human with his companion.

[22] When a few more years come,
I will go whence I'll not return.

[**17:1**] My spirit has been bruised,
My days are on the wane,
My grave is ready.[31]

[2] I attest that mockery is my lot,
And the bitterer it gets, the more my eyes cannot (bear it).[32]

[3] Pray, you[33] be my guarantor!
Who else will strike a hand (in pledge) for me?[34]

[4] You have hidden reason from their hearts.[35]
For this you will not be exalted![36]

[5] One invites over friends to share (a meal),[37]

---

30. Recall that Job at the outset (3:3) referred to himself as "man."

31. For the motif of the grave being prepared for the pious sufferer in anticipation of his death, see the Syrian (Ugarit) version of the Babylonian "Let Me Praise the Lord of Wisdom" (in Y. Cohen).

32. Reading *til'enah 'einay* for *talan 'eini* "my eye spends the night."

33. God.

34. For the gesture and language, see Proverbs 17:18 (Freedman).

35. More literally, "You have hidden their (the mockers') hearts from (being able to) reason."

36. Reading *teromam* with several scholars. Although the reference is not clear, the context suggests that it is Job who will not be exalting the deity, who has allowed his companions and others to mock him.

37. This would appear to be a gnomic saying: the companions dispense wisdom freely to others, like Job, but they keep none for themselves.

While the eyes of one's children languish.[38]

[6] He has set me up as a popular taunt;
I have become like spit in the face.[39]

[7] My eye has gone dim from anguish,
And my limbs wear away[40] like a shadow.[41]

[8–9] Even the upright rejoice[42] over this—
And the innocent exults along with the impudent,
As the righteous holds fast to his ways,
And the pure of hands becomes even bolder.

[10] And yet, may you[43] all return, pray come,
Though I won't find among you even one who is wise!

[11] My days have passed,
My plans have been rent asunder,
As have the wishes[44] of my heart.

---

38. From hunger.

39. In the light of 30:9–10, *topet* derives from Aramaic for "spittle." Job has become an object of disdain.

40. Reading *kalim* for *kullam* "all of them" (similarly Ehrlich); compare the use of *kalah* "wear away" in 19:27 and 33:21.

41. Compare 7:9, where the verb *kalah* is used of a cloud.

42. Reading *yismehu* with the addition of only the *heth*. We have the same pair of poetic synonyms (*samah* and *hit'orer*) in 31:29.

43. Reading *kullekem* "all of you" for *kullam* "all of them," seeing that the verb is second-person plural.

44. The noun is derived from the rare verb *'arash* "desire" (see Psalm 21:3). For the form *morash*, compare *mosar* "binding" from *'asar* (Job 39:5 and see the comment at 12:18).

[12] They[45] replace night with day;
(To them) light is closer than darkness.[46]

[13–14] If I measure for[47] my home in Sheol,
Arrange my bedding in the Dark,
Call out to the Pit—"You are my father!"
To the worm—"You are my mother and sister!"

[15] Where then would be my hope?
My hope—who will have seen it?

[16] Down to Sheol it will go—
Resting way down in the ground.[48]

---

45. All those who see Job's afflictions and are glad that the seemingly wicked is being punished.

46. Job feels that people who, unlike him in his present condition, prefer light to darkness have come to see his suffering as a positive—deserved affliction from God.

47. Compare "to measure with a line" in the sense of building in 38:5 (Yellin). The verb for measuring with a line is cognate to the word for "hope" in verse 15 below, producing a brilliant irony.

48. More literally, "All the way down to the dust of resting." The word *yaḥad* sometimes means just "altogether" in the sense of "entirely," as in 10:8.

BILDAD'S SECOND DISCOURSE
(18:1–21)

Bildad batters Job over his perceived disdain for traditional wisdom and then barrages him with a large dose of such wisdom, detailing the many ways in which the wicked allegedly receive their just deserts. In this Bildad resumes the theme taken up by Eliphaz in 15:17–35 and the citation of wisdom clichés that he practiced in his preceding discourse. The unstated premise in confining the discussion to the fate of the wicked is that if there is retribution for them, there will be justice for the righteous as well. The companions, however, no longer regard Job, who stubbornly clings to his innocence, as righteous.

[**18**:1] Up spoke Bildad the Shuhite and he said:

[2] "How long will you (men) put an end to discourse?[1]

---

1. Bildad begins by mocking the opening of Job's last discourse and then goes on to charge him with being crazed (verse 4). That verse 2 is a paraphrase of Job is clear from the use of the plural—a clear sign that the companions are being addressed. The phrase (literally) "ends to words (*millin*)" echoes Job's pseudo-quotation of the friends in 16:3, "end to words (*dibrei*) of wind."

Once you understand, then we can speak."[2]

[3–4] Why do you think of us as animals?
Why do we seem[3] to you brutish?[4]
He who tears himself apart in his anger—[5]
For you will the earth be made desolate?[6]
(For you) a mountain moved from its place?[7]

[5–6] The light of the wicked really does wane,
And the flame of his fire fails to glow;
The light goes dark in his habitation,
And his lamp goes out on him.[8]

[7] His pernicious[9] steps are shortened;[10]
His schemes make him stumble.[11]

[8–10] For he is caught by his feet in a net!

---

2. Job had told his friends to be silent and just listen to him (13:13).

3. Reading the singular rather than plural suffix together with the ancient Greek translation.

4. Reading *netammonu* (compare *timtem* in later Hebrew) for *nitminu*, which seems to have been taken by the Masorah as a deviant form of "we are tainted."

5. An insulting reference to Job, throwing Job's use of the phrase "(God's) anger raged" (16:9) back at him, but in a deconstructed form (separating the terms of the idiom and giving them a literal sense). Accusing Job of unrestrained anger pegs him as a fool (see 5:2).

6. Literally, "abandoned"; compare the curse in Leviticus 26:43.

7. An echo of Job in 14:18.

8. An elaboration of the conventional wisdom of Proverbs 13:9. The extinction of the hearth fire can suggest the extinction of progeny; see 2 Samuel 14:7.

9. Ironically also "his strong steps."

10. The wicked's schemes are thwarted—an echo of Job in 17:11, who complains that his plans have been frustrated.

11. Reading *wa-takshilehu* for *wa-tashlikehu* "throws him down" on the basis of Proverbs 4:12, which is alluded to here.

Wherever he walks there's a mesh!
His heel is seized by a trap;
He is held fast by a snare.
A trip-cord is buried for him in the ground,
And a catch for him by the path.

[11] Horrors terrify him all about;[12]
Causing his legs to tremble.[13]

[12] Hunger exhausts[14] his strength,
And disaster awaits his stumble![15]

[13] Someone consumes the limbs of his skin,[16]
Death's Firstborn[17] consumes his limbs

[14] He[18] is cut off from his secure habitation.[19]

---

12. Bildad's enumeration of disasters befalling the wicked recalls Eliphaz's itemization of the seven disasters from which the righteous will be saved (5:19–22).

13. Reading we-hiplitsuhu for we-hepitsuhu "they scattered him," which is inapt in context. The phrase is drawn from Isaiah 21:4; compare Job 9:6; 21:6.

14. Reading yekalleh ra'ab for yehi ra'eb "let (his strength) be hungry"; see Genesis 41:30 where the verb killah is predicated of ra'ab in the phrase "and the famine will destroy the land."

15. Compare Psalm 38:18. A different Hebrew term from that rendered "stumble" in verse 7 above.

16. "Skin" is here a metonym for the body. The subject of the consumption is not specified here—it will be specified in the next clause. There may be a superstitious reluctance to name the demonic personality.

17. "Death" is here personified—the Canaanite god Mot (Death), whose image as ravenously devouring the living is found in Habakkuk 2:5. The "firstborn" of Mot is apparently a name for a dreadful disease—like the skin disease from which Job suffers. In Biblical Hebrew "death" sometimes denotes a plague or disease (see Job 27:15).

18. The wicked.

19. "His tent." Contrast the proverbial fate of the righteous in 5:24 and 12:6.

And he's led[20] to the King of Horrors.[21]

[15] Lilith[22] will dwell in his habitation;
Sulfur'll be strewn over his estate.

[16] Below, his roots will dry out;
And above, his foliage will wither.[23]

[17] His reputation disappears from the land,
And his good name is gone from the countryside.[24]

[18] He is driven from light into darkness,
Banished from th'inhabited world.

[19] He has no son or scion among his people;[25]
Nor any remnant where he resides.

---

20. Literally, "it leads him"; the antecedent would seem to be "his schemes" in verse 7, which in Hebrew is a feminine singular like the verb in this clause (compare Ibn Ezra). The two verses are linked by the noun "step" there and its cognate verb "to lead to," used here.

21. Apparently another name for Death. The reference is to personified death or a plague demon, not necessarily the Canaanite god Mot, who is never called "king."

22. Reading *lilit* for *MBLYLW*, which is read confusedly, as one or two words, in different Masoretic traditions; the Greek reads "in his night." A feminine singular subject is required, and the ancient female demon Lilith is found together with two other terms from our verse—"sulfur" and "estate"—in the curse against Edom in Isaiah 34 (see verses 9, 13, 14; compare Driver-Gray).

23. That is, his lineage will be wiped out. Compare Amos 2:9. Bildad revisits kindred images in Job 8:11–13 and 15:32–34.

24. Job will complain of the damage his reputation suffered within his community in chapter 29.

25. Compare Isaiah 14:22. Contrast Eliphaz's forecast of progeny for Job in 5.25.

[20] Westerners are appalled at his day-of-doom,
And Easterners are seized with alarm.[26]

[21] Yes, these are the dwellings of the depraved,
The place of one who knows not El.[27]

---

26. For the correct understanding of the terms for "Westerners" and "Easterners," see 23:8; also Joel 2:20; Zechariah 14:8.

27. Some interpreters understand this verse to be spoken by the Westerners and Easterners of verse 20, but this pithy conclusion is of a piece with Bildad's prior one in 8:22; and compare the conclusion of Zophar's discourse in 20:29.

JOB'S RESPONSE TO BILDAD
(19:1–29)

Job does not yet respond directly to Bildad's brief for divine justice; he will counter his contentions in chapter 21. Here, Job expresses exasperation over his companions' harangues. They seem not to understand, as Job does, that the deity has severely wronged him. Not only does the deity seem to ignore Job's cries for justice, but he metaphorically assaults Job with a military machine. By marking Job with the stigma of God's enemy he isolates Job from family and friends. But Job conceives of two ways of vindicating himself: to make a permanent record of his claims and to present them in person before the deity.

[**19:**1] Up spoke Job and he said:

[2–3] How long will you make me anguished,
Oppressing me with words!
Ten times[1] you try to refute me,[2]

---

1. Many times; compare Numbers 14:22.
2. Compare Job 11:3.

You have no shame as you demean me.[3]

[4] For even if I've been at fault,
The fault resides within me.

[5–6] But if you keep speaking to me arrogantly,[4]
Reproaching me on account of my disgrace,
Know at least it's Eloah who's abused me,
Surrounding me with his siege-works.[5]

[7] Though I scream "I've been wronged!"[6] I receive no response;
(Though) I make an outcry, there is no justice.

[8] He has fenced in my way so I cannot pass through;[7]
He has laid darkness over my footpaths.[8]

[9] He has stripped me of my (clothes of) honor,[9]
Removed the crown from my head.[10]

[10] He has broken me down[11] and I'm going (to die).[12]

---

3. For "demean," compare Arabic *hqr* (so already M. Kimhi).

4. The verb *higdil* "to do greatly" is here an ellipsis of "to do greatly with the mouth"; compare Ezekiel 35:13.

5. Compare Job 16:13–14 above; and verses 11–12 below.

6. Compare Jeremiah 20:8 and Lamentations 3:8.

7. Compare Hosea 2:8 and especially Lamentations 3:7, 9. Job ironically inverts the sense of God's hedging Job about as a figure of protection (1:10).

8. Contrast Job 22:28.

9. Compare for example Ezekiel 16:39.

10. Compare for example Jeremiah 13:18.

11. Like a house; compare for example Psalm 52:7. Job may be alluding to the destruction of his estate and the house in which his children were killed in particular (1:19).

12. Compare for example Psalm 39:14; for the full expression, see for example Genesis 25:32.

He has uprooted my hope like a tree.[13]

[11–12] He has inflamed his anger against me,
And reckoned me one of his enemies.[14]
His troops come at me at once,
They clear an attack-road against me,
And they camp surrounding my tent.

[13–14] My relatives[15] he's kept distant from me,
And my friends[16] have withdrawn[17] from me.
My close ones have stopped (coming near),
And my familiar ones have rejected me.[18]

[15–16] Men of my household[19] and women-who-serve-me
Imagine me a stranger[20]—
In their eyes I am a foreigner.
I call to my man-servant but he does not respond—
Though I beg-him-for-mercy with my very-own mouth!

[17] My breath is foul[21] to my wife,

---

13. For the sentiment, compare Job 17:15. Job ironically twists the image in 14:7–9.

14. Compare 13:24; but there Job uses a term for "enemy" that puns on his name; here he uses a different term (*tsar*) that puns on the polysemous verb *zur* in the following four verses.

15. Literally, "my brothers."

16. Literally, "those who know me (well)."

17. Hebrew *zaru*.

18. For the theme of alienating people from the sufferer, see Psalm 31:12; 38:23; 88:9, 19; and see further Job 29.

19. Literally, "(males) who dwell in my house."

20. Hebrew *zar*.

21. Hebrew *zara*. A different verb from the better-known term for "stranger"; see for example Numbers 11:20; Psalm 78:30.

And my odor[22] to my siblings.[23]

[18] Even young-hooligans[24] detest me;
When I arise (to speak), they speak against me.

[19] All members of my circle abhor me;
Those I befriended have turned on me.

[20] My bone sticks to my skin and my flesh,[25]
I'm cemented[26] at the skin of my teeth

[21] Have compassion, compassion, you my friends!
For the hand of Eloah has afflicted me.[27]

[22] Why do you like El persecute me?
Why can't you get your fill of my flesh?[28]

---

22. Read *tsahanati* (see Joel 2:20) for *hannoti* "my pleading" (?).

23. Literally, "sons/children of my womb"—the womb in which he gestated; see Job 3:10 and the comment there. See also the introduction to this volume. This verse is strongly akin to Psalm 69:9, where "my brothers" are also called "sons of my mother." Job replaces the conventional phrase with his idiosyncratic one.

24. See Job 30:1; the same term is used of criminals in 16:11.

25. Unable to eat in his abject state, Job's bones protrude from his emaciated body; compare Psalm 102:6.

26. Compare later Aramaic *mlt*. Others tend to render: "I escape by the skin of my teeth," which doesn't mean anything. Job claims that the skin surrounding his teeth (his palate and lower jaw) is bound together so that he cannot speak. This is a conventional complaint of the pious sufferer; compare the Babylonian "Let Me Praise the Lord of Wisdom" (in Oshima). The claim is, of course, hyperbole; Job is not actually prevented from speaking.

27. Compare 1 Samuel 6:9; Ruth 1:13. The same term rendered "affected" in 1:11, 19 and 2:5.

28. To eat someone's flesh is an ancient Semitic idiom for defaming him; see Psalm 27:2; Daniel 3:8 (where the Aramaic phrase has a cognate in Babylonian).

[23–24] If only my words could be written!
If only be engraved in a record![29]
With a stylus of iron or lead,
Let them be hewn in rock as a witness![30]

[25] For I know that my redeemer[31] lives;
The respondent[32] will testify[33] on earth.[34]

[26–27] From behind my skin I look out,[35]
While in the flesh I'll see Eloah.
Something I myself will view—

---

29. The term "record" is *seper*—any written document; there may be a pun on Babylonian *siparru* "copper, brass"—producing a double entendre: would that my words were engraved with a brass tool, or in brass/copper. The same pun may be found in Isaiah 30:8, on which the Job verse may be drawing.

30. Reading *la'ed* for *la'ad* "forever." The latter reading makes sense, but the former gives more weight to the forensic framework of Job's arguments. Job wants to present his case, not to memorialize his words. The image of an inscription engraved on a high stone ledge may be modeled on the famous Behistun inscription of King Darius of Persia from the late sixth century BCE (compare Habel). The incised signs were filled with lead.

31. God; compare 16:19 and see below. The "redeemer" in this context is one who protects the wronged; see Proverbs 23:10–11. For the sense, see also Isaiah 50:8.

32. Literally, "the latter (second party)," the deity who is being sued by Job. The usage is explained by Proverbs 18:17: the "first" litigant begins a suit, and the next ("his colleague") comes to cross-examine him. "Latter" (*aharon*) here is the counterpart of the "first (litigant)" (*rishon*) there.

33. Literally, "will rise (to testify)"; see Deuteronomy 19:15.

34. Literally, "dust"; for "dust" in the sense of "the earth," see for example Job 41:25.

35. This clause is one of the most perplexing in the book. Literally it reads: "And afterwards, my skin (masculine) they flayed this (feminine)." My attempt at reconstruction is based on the assumption that, on account of the parallelism of "skin" and "flesh" (for example Job 7:5; compare 10:11; 19:20), the first clause will convey something similar to the second, which is fairly clear. The awkward combination of "they flayed this" (*nikkepu zo't*) is emended to *nishkapti* "I look out." Hebraists should note that the *Niph'al* conjugation of this verb often has an active meaning; see Judges 5:28; 2 Samuel 6:16; and Proverbs 7:6—where we find exactly the form that is restored here.

What my eyes, not a stranger's, will see.
My innards wear away within my breast.[36]

[28–29] If you are thinking,[37] "for what shall we persecute him,
What root cause[38] can we find in him?'[39]
You had better fear the sword—
For rage is a crime of the sword[40]–
You had better beware[41] of demons![42]

---

36. That is, I pine for this; compare 16:20.

37. Literally, "say (to yourselves)."

38. Literally, "root of the matter" (or legal case).

39. The received text has *bi* "in me" rather than *bo* "in him"; but only the latter reading makes sense, and it is in fact attested in several Masoratic manuscripts.

40. The passion that impels you to persecute an innocent man. The clause is unclear; but the idea that those who transgress with the sword will be chased by the sword is found for example in Leviticus 26:25. An alternate interpretation of the same words is: "For crimes by the sword are venom."

41. Literally, "know."

42. The word as traditionally read, *shaddun*, has no meaning. I read the word the way it is spelled, *shedin* "demons" (with the Aramaic plural so common in Job; compare Luzzatto). Both the "sword" and the "demon" are among the seven frightening calamities enumerated by Eliphaz in 5:20–22. Job would seem to be responding to Bildad (18:13–15), who foresees various demons afflicting the wicked. There is also a pun on *shod* "catastrophe," which is also among the seven calamities enumerated by Eliphaz.

ZOPHAR'S SECOND DISCOURSE
(20:1–29)

Like Eliphaz and Bildad before him, Zophar defends divine justice by assert-
ing that the wicked perish before their time. Whereas Job (chapters 7, 16–17)
had complained of a living death, of the brevity of his happy life, and of the
finality of the grave, Zophar insists that it is the wicked who disappear pre-
maturely, leaving open the implication that Job might be counted as wicked.
Zophar elaborates the metaphor by which the wicked "consume" ill-gotten
gain, which acts like a poison, causing them to "disgorge" it. Accordingly, the
apparent success of the wicked is ephemeral.

[**20**:1] Up spoke Zophar the Na'amathite and he said:

[2–3] It is my brooding that makes me respond—
By dint of the feelings within me.
I hear (your) lecture of refutation,
And the spirit by which I understand prompts me to speak:

[4–5] Do you not know this from forever,
Since the human was put on earth,

That the joy of the wicked is short-lived,
That the pleasure of the impudent is of the moment?

[6–7] Though his[1] summit go up to the sky,
And his head reach up to the clouds,
He will disappear like his dung for all time;
Those who've seen him[2] will say: "Where is he?"

[8–9] He'll fly off like a dream that no one can find;
He'll be banished like a vision of the night.[3]
The eye that beheld him will do so no more;
His locale will see him no longer.[4]

[10] His children will be crushed by poverty,[5]
As his hands give back his wealth.[6]

[11] His bones may be full of youthful-vigor,
But they lie down with him (dead) in the dust.

[12–14] Though evil taste sweet in his mouth,
(Though) he hide it under his tongue;
(Though) he savor[7] and not let it go,

---

1. The impudent's.
2. There is a pun on a biblical term for "excrement"— *ro'i* (Nahum 3:6; Zalcman).
3. An echo of Job 4:13.
4. Echoes of Job 7:8, 10, 21.
5. More literally, "Poverty will crush (reading *yarotsu* his sons" (compare the Latin and Syriac translations).
6. There is a pun: the term for "wealth" (*on*) can also designate one's "strength," one's progeny.
7. "Savor" (*yahmol*) echoes "like a dream" (*kahalom*) in verse 8.

And restrain it within his palate,
His food[8] will turn over in his bowels—
Serpents' venom within him.

[15] He may swallow wealth, but he will disgorge it;
El will dispossess him of it from his belly.[9]

[16] He suckles the poison of serpents,
The tongue of the viper will slay him.[10]

[17] He must never see rivulets of oil,[11]
Or streams[12] of honey and cream.

[18–19] He must restore (his) profit without swallowing it,
The amount he received without enjoying it.
For he has crushed the property[13] of the poor;[14]
Has stolen a house rather than build one.

[20–21] Because his belly will know no peace,[15]
He will not save (himself) with what he holds dear.[16]

---

8. "Food," more often "bread" (*lehem*), puns on "savors" (*yahmol*) in verse 13 and on "wealth" (*hayil*) in verse 15 and below.
9. The metaphor of consuming wealth mixes the literal (wealth, dispossess) and the figurative (swallow, disgorge).
10. As though the venom is ejected by the tongue, not the teeth.
11. Reading *yitshar* "fresh oil" for *naharei* "rivers cf." For the phrase "streams of oil," see Micah 6:7 and Job's echo of the phrase in 29:6. These delectable liquids contrast with the poisonous ones.
12. "Streams" (*nahalei*) puns on "wealth" (*hayil*) in verses 15, 18, 21.
13. Vocalizing *'azab* as a noun; compare *'izzabon* "wares" (Ezekiel 27:12, 27, 33).
14. Note the twist on verse 10 above.
15. Reading *shelew* (a noun) for *shalew* (a predicate); see Psalm 30:7.
16. Compare Psalm 39:12 (so for example Rashi).

(He has) no survivor to consume it;
Therefore his bounty will not last.[17]

[22] Though his satisfaction is complete, he's distressed;
Any sufferer's hand can overcome him.[18]

[23] On the one who fills his belly,
May he unleash his burning wrath!
And on him rain down his warfare![19]

[24–25] If he escapes from a weapon of iron,[20]
A bow of bronze will pierce him through.[21]
He[22] draws out (a sword) and it runs through the body;
The blade[23] goes right through his innards;[24]
He is stricken with fright.

[26] Darkness is in store for his protected ones;[25]
A fire unfanned[26] will consume them;[27]
Any survivor in his tent will meet disaster.[28]

---

17. For this sense of the verb *yahil*, see Psalm 10:5; there is a play on *hayil* "wealth."
18. Compare Eliphaz in 15:21.
19. Compare Psalm 11:6, where the deity "rains down" fire and sulfur on the wicked. "Warfare" (*lahum*) puns ironically on "food" (*lehem*) and "wealth" (*hayil*).
20. Such as a sword.
21. For *halap* "be pierced," see Judges 5:26. The rare verb form suggests a double meaning: a bow "will take the place" (the more common meaning of *halap*) of an unsuccessful sword.
22. God or an indefinite subject—as though to say, "A sword is drawn . . ."
23. An ellipsis of "the lightning blade (of a sword)"; see Deuteronomy 32:41.
24. Literally, "comes out from his gall."
25. Apparently his family; see Psalm 83:4.
26. A supernatural fire, like the one that annihilated Job's flocks and servants (1:16).
27. Literally, "him" (in Job singular and plural are not always distinguished).
28. Reading *yeira'* as a passive (*Niph'al*; so D. Kimhi).

[27] The heavens will reveal his crime;
And the earth will rise against him.

[28] A torrent[29] will sweep away[30] his house—
Inundation on the day of his[31] anger.

[29] This is the wicked man's portion from Elohim,
The allotment that El has declared for him.

---

29. Reading *yubal* for *yebul* "crop"; see Jeremiah 17:8.
30. Reading *yiggal* (*Niph'al* of *gll*) for *yigel* "go into exile"; see Amos 5:24 (said of water).
31. The deity's.

JOB'S RESPONSE TO ZOPHAR
(21:1–34)

Job bids his companions understand that his complaint is directed to the deity, who, to his mind, causes him, a righteous man, to suffer and at the same time causes the wicked to prosper. Taking his cue from Jeremiah (12:1–2) and Habakkuk (chapter 1), Job refutes Zophar's claims in the preceding discourse to the effect that the wicked die prematurely, lose their ill-gotten wealth, and have no legacy. In the course of his argument, Job counters earlier claims by Eliphaz and Bildad as well.

[**21:1**] Up spoke Job and he said:

[**2–3**] Listen oh listen to my words,
And let them be your (words of) consolation!
Bear with me while I speak;
Then after I speak, you can blather.[1]

---

1. Reading *ta'legu* (adding the plural suffix), a metathesis of *tal'igu* "you mock," which ordinarily takes the preposition *le*-with object; see above at 11:3.

93

[4] Is this complaint of mine with a human?
Should I not lose patience[2] over an evil?[3]

[5] Face me and be still,[4]
And set your hands over your mouths!

[6] When I call (the evil) to mind, I am shaken;
My flesh has been seized by trembling.

[7] Why do the wicked live on and live well,[5]
Grow old[6] and gain in power and wealth?[7]

[8–9] Their seed[8] is steadfastly before them,
Their offspring ever before their eyes.[9]
Their homesteads are at peace[10] without dread,
With no rod of Eloah's (anger) over them.[11]

[10] His[12] bull never fails to impregnate,

---

2. Literally, "should my spirit not be short," an idiom.

3. Reading *meroa*' "on account of evil" for *maddua*' "why?," which cannot follow the interrogative *'im*. The letters *d* and *r* are nearly identical.

4. So the Aramaic translation. The verb *sh-m-m* connotes desolation; it puns on "set, put" (*simu*) in the next line.

5. Thriving, prospering is a nuance of "live" known in Old Aramaic and compare Psalms 22:27; 69:33.

6. And strong. The nuance of "old" is particularly found in Aramaic.

7. Hebrew *ḥayil* denotes "wealth" in Zophar's speech (20:15, 18, 21) but always connotes "strength" as well.

8. Children.

9. The phrase *'immam* "with them," which seems redundant in the first line of this couplet, should probably be read as part of the second line (Kahana); compare Isaiah 65:23.

10. Compare Eliphaz's assurance to Job in 5:24.

11. Job counters Zophar's assertions in 20:23–25.

12. The wicked now in the singular.

His cow calves without any losses.

[11] They[13] let their young run rampant[14] like sheep,
And their children prance around.

[12] They raise (their voices)[15] with[16] hand-drum and lyre,
And take pleasure at the sound of the flute.

[13–16] They end[17] their days in bounty,[18]
And descend[19] to Sheol at ease,[20]
Though they say to El: "Turn away from us!
We are not interested in knowing your ways.[21]
Why should we serve Shaddai?
What do we gain by imploring[22] him?
Not in his hands[23] is our bounty,[24]

---

13. The wicked.

14. "Young running rampant" is the same term as "hooligans" in 19:18.

15. An expression for singing in Isaiah 42:11.

16. Reading be- for ke- with ancient translations and some Masoretic manuscripts.

17. Reading the Qere (tradition of reading) rather than the Ketib (written version) with Saadia Gaon and others; compare 36:11. The expression billa "wear out" of the Ketib has a negative connotation.

18. Contrast Zophar's claim in 20:21.

19. Vocalizing yeḥatu from the regular Aramaic verb for descending; it is generally understood this way.

20. Vocalizing beroga' instead of the received berega' "in a moment"—a punning reply to Zophar in 20:5. Compare Deuteronomy 28:65; Isaiah 28:12; Jeremiah 6:16.

21. The opposite of what the righteous will desire; see Isaiah 58:2, which is quoted here almost verbatim.

22. Compare Jeremiah 7:16.

23. Reading beyadaw for beyadam "in their hands." (For the reading of this verse I am indebted to Alexander Rofé.)

24. Reading tubenu for tubam "their bounty" (the letters nw when written adjacent to each other look like final m; see at 8:8).

The scheme of the wicked is far from him."[25]

[17–18] How often does the lamp of the wicked wane?[26]
And their ruin overcome them?
(How often) does he dispense disaster in his anger?
(How often) are they like straw in the wind,
And like chaff that a wind sweeps away?[27]

[19–21] (How often) does Eloah store up his misfortune for his[28]
    sons,
Pay him (thus) his retribution—and he knows it?
(How often) do his eyes witness his downfall,[29]
Does he drink from Shaddai's wrathful venom?[30]
For what interest has he in his household after him—
When the number of his months has been halved?[31]

[22] Can one teach awareness[32] to El,
When he is judging from the heights?[33]

---

25. Reading *mennu* for *menni* "from me"—beyond the deity's notice. Compare Eliphaz's rejoinder in 22:18. The received text does not make sense as an observation of Job's.

26. A direct refutation of Bildad in 18:5—and Proverbs 13:9.

27. A denial of conventional wisdom, as in Psalm 1:4.

28. The wicked, now in the singular.

29. Reading *pid* "catastrophe" (see Job 12:5 and elsewhere) for otherwise unknown *kid*; compare Rashi.

30. For the expression and image, see for example Isaiah 51:17.

31. When he is nearing death.

32. "Knowledge" of what transpires among humans; see Eliphaz's paraphrase of this verse in 22:13.

33. Too high in the heavens to be aware of earthly doings; see 22:13–14 and Job in 3:23.

[23–24] This one[34] dies wholly hale,[35]
Completely at ease and at rest.
His buckets are full of milk,[36]
The marrow of his bones refreshed.

[25–26] While this one[37] dies in a bitter spirit,
Never having eaten sweet bounty.
They lie in the dust together,
And maggots cover them both.[38]

[27–28] See, I know what you are thinking,
The arguments you contemplate[39] against me.
You will say, "Where's the house of the beneficent?
And where is the home[40] the wicked dwell in?"[41]

[29–30] Have you not questioned wayfarers?
Their indications you can hardly deny:[42]
That on the day of disaster the wicked is spared,
On the day of fury they will be delivered.[43]

---

34. The wicked. Job reasserts his contention in 9:22.
35. In Job health, like integrity, is figured by wholeness.
36. Possibly a metaphor for testes full of semen (Gordis, *Book of Job*).
37. The righteous.
38. Compare Isaiah 14:11.
39. Reading *tahmosu* "you imagine" (known from Syriac, with many commentators) for *tahmosu* "you do violence."
40. Literally, "the tent."
41. That is, you will claim there is a difference in the lot of the good and the bad.
42. Compare Deuteronomy 32:27.
43. Compare Isaiah 55:12.

[31] Who will confront (the wicked) with his ways?[44]
For what he has done, who will pay him his due?

[32–33] (Who will tell him) he'll be delivered to the grave,
That a tomb will keep watch over him?[45]
That the clods of the stream will be his comfort;[46]
That he will draw after him every man,
As countless ones (went) before him?

[34] Why do you console me with windy breath?
Why do your responses remain[47] futile?[48]

---

44. Literally, "tell to his face his ways."
45. Reading 'alaw "over him" (Ball).
46. Literally, "will be sweet for him."
47. Reading a plural verb (nish'aru).
48. Reading 'amal for ma'al "betrayal"; see the similar usage in 16:2.

ELIPHAZ'S THIRD DISCOURSE
(22:1–30)

Eliphaz reacts to Job's argument that the wicked thrive because God is too remote to know or care. First, Eliphaz mocks Job's insistence that the deity is charging him with undisclosed crimes and using them as a basis for punishing him (see especially chapter 13). Eliphaz's parody of the alleged divine indictment is virtually the converse of the characterization of the righteous person in Ezekiel 18:5–9. Then Eliphaz contends that what Job regards as the deity's remoteness in high heaven gives him a vantage point from which to enact justice. The wicked, he claims, lose their good fortune, and Job should be able to see that. Far from writing Job off, Eliphaz again advises him to restore his relationship with God and enjoy divine succor.

[**22:1**] Up spoke Eliphaz the Teimanite and he said:

[2–3] Does a man bring benefit to El?
Can (even) the clever bring benefit to him?[1]

---

1. Perhaps Eliphaz is making this inference on the basis of Job's complaint in 10:14–15.

Does Shaddai have an interest in your being just?
Does he make a profit from your integrity?[2]

[4] Is it from fear of you[3] that he should accuse you,
That he should join a lawsuit with you:[4]

[5–7, 9][5] "You see, your evildoing is great!
There is no end to your crimes!
For you seize-collateral from your brothers without cause;
And you strip the clothes off the naked.
No water do you give the weary to drink;
And from the hungry you withhold food.
Widows you've dismissed empty-handed;
And you push back the arms of the fatherless."[6]

[10–11] That is why all around you are traps;
And why sudden dread overwhelms you.
Your light goes dark[7]—so you cannot see;

---

2. Literally, "Or is there a profit (for him) if you make your ways whole?" Compare 4:6.

3. A pun: the term for "fear" is identical to that for "reverence" in 4:6, where it is associated with Job's "integrity."

4. What follows (through verse 11) is a parody of the charges Job imagines the deity is making against him, on the basis of which he believes he is being punished by God (Tur-Sinai). The charges are too extreme to be serious—violations of the norms set forth in Exodus 22:21–26 and elsewhere. Eliphaz is mocking Job's claim that the deity is paying him undue attention. The norms entailed here are traditional responsibilities of a just leader, reflected for example in the North Canaanite (Ugaritic) epic of Kirta.

5. Verse 8 is out of place, interrupting the mock tirade. It was apparently miscopied here because the scribe saw the word "arm" in verse 9 and mistakenly copied verse 8, which also features the word "arm." Realizing his error, the scribe returned to verse 9 and continued copying. Verse 8 makes sense following verse 14.

6. Reading second-person *tedakke'* with several ancient translations, in accord with the preceding verb forms instead of the third-person (and incongruent singular) *yedukke'*.

7. Reading *'oreka hashak* for *'o hoshek* "or darkness," based on 18:6, style, and the Old Greek translation.

And a downpour of water blankets you.[8]

[12] Truly, Eloah is in highest heaven;
At the top[9] of the lofty stars![10]

[13–14] But you have said: "What does El know?
Can he enact justice from behind foggy cloud?[11]
The clouds are his blind, so he cannot see,
As he walks about the rim of the sky.

[8] So the man of the arm,[12] his is the earth;
And the (man of) raised face[13] inhabits it."[14]

[15–16] Don't you observe[15] the ways of the depraved,[16]
That men of iniquity have trod—
Who have been severed[17] before their time,
Their foundation swept away by a stream?

---

8. Said for example of the drowning of the Egyptians in Exodus 14:28; 15:5, 10.

9. Literally, "head." The received text begins the line with "And look!" which interrupts the syntactic sequence. The scribe apparently began writing "And the top" (w-r-'-shi, but wrote a he instead of a shin (w-r-'-h, "and look!") and, without erasing the mistaken writing, wrote the desired word correctly (compare Budde). The scribal habit of not erasing errors, of simply continuing to copy the correct text, is deeply rooted in the ancient Near East and in the Bible. See note 5 above.

10. There are two implications to Eliphaz's point: God is too elevated to pay mind to Job in the way Job imagines; yet on account of his elevation he can see everything—contrary to Job's assertions. Compare Psalm 33:12–13.

11. A direct rejoinder to Job's assertion in 21:22; and compare 3:23.

12. Power.

13. The recipient of the powerful's favor, the privileged; see 2 Kings 5:1; Isaiah 3:3.

14. Compare Job's assertion in 9:24.

15. There is a double sense: "observe" and "maintain." Does Job not realize what happens to the wicked? Is he beginning to behave like them?

16. Reading 'awwalim for 'olam "primeval" (ways); see 18:21 (compare Hayyut).

17. Cut off from the land of the living (see Isaiah 53:8). Compare Aramaic qetam "lop off" (Kahana).

[17–18] Who say to El: "Turn away from us!
What can Shaddai do to us?"[18]
When he filled their houses with bounty,
When the wicked's plan was remote from him?[19]

[19–20] The righteous see (this) and rejoice,
And the innocent mocks them:
"I swear[20] their substance[21] is destroyed,
And their earnings consumed by fire!"

[21] Pray be solicitous of him[22] and be whole (again)!
Thus will the bountiful come your way.

[22] Pray accept the instruction of his mouth,
And fix his teachings in your heart!

[23–25] If you return to Shaddai you will be rebuilt—[23]
(If) you keep depravity far from your tent;[24]
And treat choice-gold as (no more than) soil,
And rocks in the stream as the gold of Ophir—[25]

---

18. Reading *lanu* for *lamo* "to him/to them" with some of the ancient versions. Eliphaz is echoing Job in 21:14–15.

19. Reading *menu* for *menni* "from me" with the ancient Greek. Eliphaz is echoing Job in 21:16.

20. An oath formula.

21. Reading *qimam* for *qimanu* "our substance"; the final *m* was misread as the sequence *nw* (a ligature; see for example on 15:18).

22. "Be solicitous" is the same verb rendered "benefit" above in verse 2.

23. An echo of Job's mock wisdom in 12:14.

24. Echoing Zophar in 11:14.

25. Famed for its gold (Isaiah 13:12); imported from somewhere south of the land of Israel (see 1 Kings 9:28). "Ophir" puns on *'apar* "dust, dirt" in the preceding line; "rocks" puns on "choice gold." For *shat* with preposition in the sense of "treat as," see for example Jeremiah 3:19.

If Shaddai will be your choicest-gold,[25]
And the silver that sparkles[27] for you;

[26–27] Then when you entreat Shaddai,[28]
And lift your face up to Eloah (in prayer),
When you appeal to him, he will hear you;
And you will pay your vows in full.

[28] Then when you issue a resolution.
Light will shine o'er your paths.[29]

[29–30] For he brings low the high and haughty,[30]
And the one of lowered eye[31] he saves.
Since El rescues the innocent,[32]
You'll be rescued[33] for the cleanness of your hands.

---

26. There is a double sense: if the deity will be "your fortress."

27. Derived from the verb "shine" in Job 10:22.

28. For the usage of this verb, compare 27:10; also Psalm 37:4.

29. Contrast Job's perspective in 19:8 and verse 11 above.

30. The received text has: "For they are low, and you say, 'back/body,'" which is obviously corrupted. In accordance with the parallel line, in which the deity is clearly the subject, the present line must have the deity as its subject. The conjunction of illuminating the devotee's path and bringing the haughty low is found in Psalm 18:28–29. In view of verse 28 there and Isaiah 2:11–12, where we find the phrase *kol geeh wa-ram*, "every haughty and high (person)," I read (with Ginsberg, compare Ball): *ki hishpil 'et ram we-geeh.*

31. The humble, the meek.

32. "Innocent" is a forensic derivation from the basic meaning of "clean." The received text has: "He rescues the un-innocent/unclean," which makes no sense here. For *'i naqi* "un-innocent" (the negative *'i* is postbiblical) read *'el naqi* "El (rescues) the innocent" (for example Ball). Ibn Janah (11th c.) in *The Book of Roots* realized a letter must be supplied.

33. Reading *we-nimlatta* "you will be rescued" for *we-nimlat* "he is rescued."

JOB'S RESPONSE TO ELIPHAZ
(23:1–24:17, 24:25)

Eliphaz would have Job believe that the deity has no interest in responding to Job's lawsuit but would welcome any gesture of reconciliation. Job explains that because his suffering is profound, he feels compelled to confront the deity with his complaints. However, as before (see chapters 9 and 13), he is intimidated. Eliphaz's mockery of Job's lawsuit he answers by insisting it is no joke: the wicked perpetrate the very crimes delineated in the parody of divine charges Eliphaz enumerates—and the deity indulges them. The seeming success of the wicked, as Job had indicated in his last discourse, calls divine justice into question no less than his own innocent suffering. Following Job's argument is sometimes tricky because he shifts back and forth between the wicked and their victims without explicit indication.

[**23:**1] Up spoke Job and he said:

[2] My complaint is no less bitter today;[^1]

---

[^1]: See 7:11.

His hand[2] weighs down on my moaning.

[3–5] If he would let me know how to find him,
I would come before his seat.
I would lay before him my lawsuit,[3]
And fill my mouth with accusations.
I would know the words he would answer me,
And discern what he would say to me.

[6–7] Would he argue with me by force of might?[4]
No, he would make his own case against me![5]
There[6] the upright would have a hearing[7] with him,
And I would truly[8] get[9] my day-in-court.[10]

[8–9] But east I go, and he is not (there);
And west, but I do not discern him.
North, in his concealment[11] I do not grasp (him);[12]
He cloaks (himself) south, so I do not see (him).

---

2. "Hand of God" denotes a plague or calamity in ancient Semitic, and compare for example Exodus 9:3; 1 Samuel 5:9. The expression "the hand of the Lord weighed down upon" conveys an affliction of the enemy in 1 Samuel 5:6. Reading *yado* "his hand" for *yadi* "my hand" with the Greek and Syriac versions.

3. Compare 13:18.

4. What Job feared in 13:20–21.

5. The verb *sim* "set" is an ellipsis of the Joban phrase "set (make) a legal case" in 5:8; this is confirmed by Elihu's elaboration of the same ellipsis in 34:23.

6. At the deity's seat of justice (verse 3).

7. A technical term for legal disputation in Job, related to "accusations" in verse 4 above.

8. Comparing a similar Arabic expression (Kopf) and see 1 Samuel 15:29.

9. Used of an animal snatching its prey in Isaiah 5:29.

10. Reading *mishpati* "judgment, litigation" for *m'-shopti* "from my judge."

11. The verb *'asah* in the sense of "cover" is an Arabism.

12. The verb has a double sense: "see" (short form of *hazah*) and "grasp" (*'ahaz*).

[10] Yet he knows what path is mine;
Were he to test me, I'd emerge like (pure) gold.

[11–12] My foot has held fast[13] to his course,
His path I have kept and not strayed.
The command of his lips I have never neglected,[14]
In my bosom[15] I've stored the words of his mouth.

[13–14] Once he's chosen (a fate),[16] who can reverse it?
Once his heart desires, he enacts it.
When he's made complete my current lot,
He still has in hand much more of the same.

[15–16] That is why[17] I'd be shaken in his presence:
I would apprehend—and be afraid of him.
For El has weakened my resolve;[18]
And Shaddai has made me shaken.

[17] Yet I am not devastated by gloom,[19]
Nor has darkness covered my face.[20]

---

13. The same verb as "grasp" (see verse 9).
14. Compare *mush* "relegate to oblivion" in Zechariah 3:9 and Akkadian *meshu* "to forget" (Held, "Studies").
15. Reading *beheqi* "in my bosom" for *mehuqqi* "more than my allotment" with the Greek and Latin versions and in conformity with the similar expression in Psalm 119:11.
16. Reading *bahar* "he has chosen" for *be'ehad* "in one" (*d* and *r* are often confused). Compare the pairing of verbs in Psalm 132:13.
17. Job's rejoinder to Eliphaz in 22:10.
18. Literally, "softened my heart"—demoralized me.
19. Literally, "by the face of gloom, darkness."
20. The language is somewhat unclear. For *mippanai* "from before me" in the second line read perhaps *panai* "my face" (with some versions).

[24:1] Why have times (of wrath) not been stored by Shaddai?[21]
(Why) have those who know him not foreseen his days (of wrath)?[22]

[2–4] They[23] pull back boundary-lines.[24]
Steal flocks and graze them (as their own).
They drive off the orphan's donkey,
Take in pledge the widow's ox.[25]
They turn the needy off the road;
The poor of the land are forced to hide.

[5–6] Wild asses go to the wilderness for their wage,
They look for prey in the desert, food for their young.[26]
They[27] harvest in a field not their own,[28]
They collect the remains[29] of the rich man's[30] orchard.

---

21. Job accuses the deity of failing to stock an arsenal of punishments for the wicked—whose activities he will describe in what follows. Compare Deuteronomy 32:34–35. For "times (of disaster)," compare Psalm 10:1.

22. See 20:28. The "Day of the Lord" is a well-known prophetic notion, a time at which the deity unleashes punishment. The wicked seem to show no fear of retribution.

23. The wicked.

24. For this crime, see Deuteronomy 19:14.

25. For this crime, see Deuteronomy 24:6.

26. The general syntax and sense of this difficult verse are illuminated by comparison with Psalm 104:23. The phrase *lo* "for him" is apparently dittography.

27. The poor of the land (verse 4). Just as undomesticated animals must fend for themselves in the wild, the poor must find sustenance in available fields.

28. Reading *belilo* "his fodder" as two words—*beli lo*, with several ancient translations, and see 18:15.

29. The unique verb *liqqesh* is related to late crops (in the tenth-century BCE Hebrew inscription known as the Gezer Calendar) and late rain (*malqosh*)—they come only after the harvest and collect what remains.

30. Reading (with several commentators) *'ashir* "wealthy" for *rasha'* "wicked." There is no reason to single out the wicked as the owner of the orchard.

[7–8] They lie down naked at night for lack of clothing—
They have no cover against the cold.
They are soaked by mountain rain,
And for lack of shelter hug the rocks.[31]

[9] They[32] rob the orphan from the breast,[33]
And seize in pledge the child[34] of the poor.

[10–11] They[35] walk about naked for lack of clothing,
And though they starve, they must carry sheaves of grain.
When the olives drop,[36] they press (them);
They must trample the winepress though they thirst!

[12] From within the town the mortals howl,
And the throats of the wounded cry for help;
But Eloah does not hear (their) prayer.[37]

[13] These are among the rebellious of the land,[38]

---

31. Compare the language of Isaiah 25:4.

32. The wicked.

33. Hebrew "orphan" has the narrower meaning of "fatherless"—he may well have a mother.

34. Reading 'ul "infant, child" for the preposition 'al (so Malbim and others).

35. The poor.

36. Reading binshor zetim "in the dropping of olives" (compare Anat) for bein shurotam "between their rows," which provides no context or antecedent. The verb nashar is the Aramaic and Late Hebrew equivalent of nashal, said of olives in Deuteronomy 28:40.

37. Reading with some versions and traditions: yishma' tepillah for yasim tiplah "(does not) treat as slander." The reading is supported by Elihu's echo in 34:28; and compare Job in 27:9.

38. Reading 'arets "land" with the ancient Greek for 'or "light." These rebels against the ways of God are enumerated in the following verses. They specifically violate the sixth, seventh, and eighth of the Ten Commandments, in that order.

Who do not acknowledge his[39] ways,
And do not dwell in his paths.

[14a-b] At the light (of day) rises the murderer—
He will slay the poor and the needy,

[15] The eye of the adulterer keeps watch for dusk,
Saying, "No eye will observe me";
So he places his face under cover.

[14c, 16–17] And at night the thief walks about;[40]
He breaks into houses in the dark.
During the day they[41] seal themselves up.
They do not care[42] for the light.
For all of them daybreak is deep-shade,[43]
For they[44] know well the terrors of deep-shade.

[25][45] If it is not so, then who can prove me false?
Who can dismiss my words as nothing?

---

39. God's.

40. This line from the end of verse 14 apparently belongs here. Reading *yehallek garab* "walks about a thief"—or in Aramaic: *yehak ganab*—for *yehi ke-ganab* "he will be like a thief" (Dhorme and others).

41. The thieves.

42. For this sense of *yada'* "to know," see the comment on 9:21.

43. Night is day for the wicked; see Job 38:15.

44. Reading plural *yakkiru* for the singular.

45. For verses 18–24, see what immediately follows.

A SECONDARY RESPONSE TO JOB
(24:18-24)

Between 24:17 and 24:25 is a passage that challenges interpreters with its unusually difficult language and text. Some take it as the continuation of Job's description of the wicked and the deity's support of their misconduct— but some verses (such as 20) appear to pronounce an ill fate on the wicked. Others take the passage to express Job's wish for the wicked to be cursed and punished—but the verb forms do not express a wish. It is here understood that the passage is meant to provide the refutation that Job provokes in 24:25; it is inserted secondarily after 24:17. Although it is tempting to see in this passage (as some do) a section of Zophar's missing third discourse, it may have been composed by a later hand, like the Elihu speeches. Any translation of this passage must remain provisional.

[**24**:18] He[1] floats-lightly upon the water;[2]

---

1. The criminal.
2. The point is, he can be seen, in spite of his efforts to act under cover. See Elihu's elaboration of this theme in 34:21–22. For the image, compare Hosea 10:7.

His plot of land is accursed;[3]
He cannot make headway through the orchards.[4]

[19] Parching and heat remove[5] the snow water;
(Thus) does Sheol (remove) those who sin.

[20] He can forget mercy;[6]
His hope is the worm;[7]
He will no more be remembered;
And wrongdoing will be broken like a tree.

[21] He mates[8] with a barren woman—she will not give birth.
(He mates with) a widow—it will do him no good.

[22] He may draw along mighty men[9] with his strength;
But when he acts,[10] he will find his life insecure.[11]

[23] He[12] will allow him to feel safe, supported.

---

3. "Floats-lightly" puns on "accursed," which in turn partially echoes "plot (of land)."
4. He can run, but he cannot hide. Orchards serve as a hiding place in Judges 21:20–21.
5. Literally, "steal."
6. Reading *rahamim* "mercy" for *rehem* "womb, woman," taking the extra *m* from the beginning of the following word. Compare the ancient translations.
7. Reading *tiqwato* "his hope" for *metaqo* "is sweet to him" (which does not agree in gender with the word for "worm," which metonymically represents the grave (similarly, Szczygiel). Compare Job 34:15.
8. For this usage, compare Proverbs 29:3.
9. The Greek translation reads *'ebyonim* "the needy."
10. Literally, "stands up."
11. Reading *hayyaw* "his life" for *hayyin,* the Aramaic form of "life"; so several ancient translations. This fate alludes to the curse in Deuteronomy 28:56.
12. God.

But his eyes are on their[13] paths.

[24] They[14] lift but a little, and they[15] are gone;
They lower, and they shrivel like grass;[16]
And they wither like the head of a stalk.

---

13. Of the wicked. Compare the echo in Job 34:21.

14. God's eyes.

15. The wicked. Reading *we'einam* "and they are not" for *we'einenu* "and he is not" (with some ancient translations); as seen above (for example at 15:18) , the combination *nw* and the letter (final) *m* are easily confused.

16. *Kol* is a term for "grass" known from Arabic. Compare the Aramaic translation from Qumran; so R. Meyuhhas and some modern scholars.

BILDAD'S THIRD DISCOURSE
(25:1–26:14)

Bildad returns to Job's claim (4:12–21) to have received esoteric knowledge about the deity's conduct of the world and, more specifically, his attitude toward humankind. As Bildad explains, God's control of creation prompts both awe and dread. Job is therefore in no position to comprehend God's ways. The segments of this discourse have somehow been copied out of order in the received Hebrew text. The proper sequence is reconstructed with the aid of such clues as singular address (necessarily to Job), introduction to a quotation (26:4), a paraphrase of Job (25:4–6), and thematic associations (see the introduction to this volume).

[25:1] Up spoke Bildad the Shuhite and he said:

[26:2–3] How do you offer help without power?[1]
How do you save with an arm lacking strength?

---

1. The singular address must belong to a companion, not to Job, who addresses his companions in the plural.

How do you give counsel without wisdom,
Imparting so much sage knowledge?

[**26:4**] Whose words are you revealing?
Whose breath comes forth from you:[2]

[**25:4–6**] "How can a mortal be righteous before El?[3]
How can a man born of woman be innocent[4]?
If the moon cannot shine brightly[5] enough,
And the stars are not pure in his eyes,[6]
Then all the less a mortal, a maggot;
(All the less) a son of a human, a worm!"[7]

[**25:2–3**] Dominion and dread are his.
He makes peace in his heights.
Is there a number to his celestial troops?[8]
On whom does his daylight[9] not rise?

[**26:5–6**] The shades of the dead writhe
Under the sea and its dwellers.[10]
Sheol is naked before him,

---

2. An introduction to direct discourse, in this case a parody of the words of the spirit, quoted by Job in 4:17–19. Eliphaz had done the same in 15:14–16.

3. Compare Job 4:17; 15:14.

4. Literally, "be pure, clean." Compare Job 15:14.

5. The *aleph* only indicates a vowel; the form is a *Hiph'il* of *h-l-l.*

6. Compare Job 15:15.

7. Compare Job 4:19, where the human is merely one born in dust, not a worm.

8. A figure for the stars; see Judges 5:20; Isaiah 40:26.

9. An ironic contrast to the "daylight," which is night, to which the murderer "rises" in Job 24:14; compare 38:15.

10. The netherworld (see the next line) is located here beneath the sea. Compare Isaiah 26:19, where the "shades" "dwell" in the dust.

Abaddon[11] has no garment to cover it.

[7–8] He stretches Mount Zaphon[12] o'er the Chaos,[13]
He suspends the earth over nothing at all.
He bundles up water in his clouds,[14]
And none bursts under its weight.

[9–10] He encloses[15] the face[16] of the new moon,[17]
He spreads[18] over it his clouds.[19]
He draws a border round the face of the water,[20]
At the limit where light meets darkness.

[11] The pillars supporting the sky shudder[21]
Stunned by the blast of his rebuke.[22]

---

11. The realm of oblivion, another name for the netherworld; see also Job 28:22.

12. The Mount Olympus of Canaanite mythology; see Psalm 48:3, where Jerusalem, seat of Israel's God, is identified with the seat of the Canaanite pantheon. The verb "stretch" is conventionally used of the sky (as in Job 9:8), but it is the land, not the sky, that is set over the watery chaos, and the context here makes a reference to land fairly clear.

13. The watery chaos of Genesis 1:2.

14. Compare Proverbs 30:4.

15. Compare later Aramaic usage in the sense of "to shut."

16. The surface; compare the surface of the water in the following couplet.

17. Reading keseh with no change in spelling; see Psalm 81:4. Ancient translations and most moderns read "throne," but that word is properly spelled ks' (not ksh), and the sense of "throne" is inapt in context; compare the image in Job 9:7. Traditional commentators interpret "throne" figuratively as the heavens, the throne of the deity.

18. The well-known Hebrew verb paras (compare Psalm 105:39) has a superfluous z at the end. Perhaps a stray letter, like a w from a spelling pwrs, was mistakenly inserted here; or there is contamination from the z at the end of m'hz in the preceding line.

19. Compare Job 9:7.

20. An act from the time of creation; see Proverbs 8:27.

21. An Aramaism; the verb r-p-p translates the "trembling" of the "pillars" in the Aramaic translation to Job 9:6.

22. The noun "rebuke" is used of the deity's primordial suppression of the sea and issues from a "blast of his nostrils"; see Psalm 18:16.

[12–13] Using his power he aroused and stilled[23] the sea,
And using his skill he smote Rahab;[24]
Using his wind he put Yamm[25] in his net;[26]
His hand pierced the Elusive[27] Serpent.

[14] Now these are only the outskirts[28] of his ways.[29]
Yet what hint of a word do we hear of them?[30]
Who can apprehend his mighty thunder?[31]

---

23. The verb is artfully ambiguous. Contrast *raga'* in Isaiah 51:15 and Jeremiah 31:34 ("arouse") with *heraga'* in Jeremiah 47:6 ("be stilled").

24. An Israelite name for the primeval sea monster; see Job 9:13.

25. The Canaanite sea god and sea monster of Israelite mythology; see Job 3:8; 7:12; 38:8–9.

26. The Hebrew is unintelligible as written. Following Tur-Sinai, many now divide the word *shamayim*, "sky," in the middle and read: *sam yam sipro*, "he put Yamm into his net," which has a precise parallel in the scene of combat between the Babylonian storm-god Marduk and the old sea goddess Ti'awat in the epic myth *Enuma Elish*. The Hebrew *sipro* "his net" reflects the Babylonian word for "net," *saparru*, which is cognate to Hebrew *siprah* "bag" in Psalm 56:9 and perhaps the word *shaprir* "net(?)" in Jeremiah 43:10.

27. Literally, "fleeing"; it is an archaic epithet of the primordial sea monster in Canaanite (Ugaritic) mythology and in Isaiah 27:1.

28. Compare Job 28:24.

29. Like the tip of the iceberg.

30. More literally, "But what hint of a word is heard of it?"

31. Thunder is often understood as the voice of the deity; for example Psalm 18:14.

JOB'S RESPONSE TO BILDAD
(27:1–23)

Job reiterates his honesty and integrity, reminding his companions that were he truly impious, he would not deign to be heard by the deity. Irritated by his friends' preaching, he quotes back at them the nonsense they have been saying. (The fact that Job's paraphrase of the companions' message is marked in the rhetoric has not been discerned by commentators, who tend to attribute verses 13–23 to the missing response of Zophar.)

[27:1] Job again took up his discourse and he said:

[2] By the life of El, he has set aside my charges!
Shaddai has embittered my life!

[3–4] So long as there is life-breath within me,
And in my nostrils Eloah's spirit,
I swear that my lips will speak nothing corrupt,
And my tongue will utter no deceit.

[5–7] God forbid[1] I declare you[2] in the right—
Not till I expire!
I will not set aside my integrity.
I hold fast to my righteousness;
I will not let it go.
My heart[3] has never been impudent (saying):
"May my enemy be like the wicked,
And my opponent like the corrupt!"[4]

[8–10] For what hope will the impudent gain
If he turns to Eloah in prayer?[5]
Will his outcry be heard by El
When he's overcome by disaster?
Can he entreat Shaddai,
Or call on Eloah at will?[6]

[11] I will instruct you in the powers of El;
What Shaddai has in hand I will not conceal.

[12] Since you have yourselves all been witness,[7]

---

1. For the full phrase, including the name of the deity, see 1 Samuel 24:6.

2. My companions.

3. The ultimate source of speech; see at 8:10.

4. Characteristically, Job had never employed a curse, even against his enemies. Compare his concern that his children might curse the deity in their hearts in a light-headed moment (1:5).

5. Literally, "if he raises his spirit to Eloah." Assuming an *aleph* has been dropped, I read *yissa' le'loah*; see Psalm 25:1; Lamentations 3:41; and compare Job 22:26 (so Ball, *The Book of Job*). The received reading *yeishel* yields interpretations that do not comport with the context.

6. Literally, "at any time."

7. Literally, "have seen"; Job's companions are aware of his situation.

How could you be spewing such nonsense?[8]

[13] "This is the wicked man's portion from El,
The allotment that villains[9] receive from Shaddai:[10]

[14–15] Should he[11] have many children—the sword is their fate;[12]
And as for his offspring, they will want for food.[13]
Those who survive him will be buried in a plague;[14]
And their widows will not mourn them.[15]

[16–17] If he amasses silver like dirt,
And stores up garments like soil,
He will store up—but the righteous will wear;
And the silver—the innocent will receive.[16]

[18] Like a spider[17] he builds his house;

---

8. More literally, "breathing out such windy-speech." For the verb and its usage, compare Jeremiah 23:16, where it is said of false prophets. The verb introduces direct discourse here—as Job quotes and paraphrases the kinds of things his friends have been saying.

9. "Brigands" in 6:23.

10. This verse is an almost verbatim quotation of Zophar in 20:29, a fact that supports the thesis that Job is here citing what he regards as the absurd contentions of his friends.

11. The wicked.

12. Literally, "to the sword"; compare Jeremiah 15:2.

13. Compare Bildad in 18:16, 19; Zophar in 20:4–11, 21, 26; Eliphaz in 22:15–16, 20.

14. For "death" in the sense of plague, see for example Exodus 10:17; Jeremiah 15:2.

15. Compare Psalm 78:64.

16. More literally, "receive as a portion," echoing verse 13 above. For a similar sentiment, compare Zophar in 20:18–21.

17. Two letters have fallen out of the word 'akabish "spider," leaving the word 'ash "moth"; the correct reading is supported by the ancient Greek and Syriac translations; and compare Saadia and R. Meyuhhas, among others. For the image of a flimsy spider's web, see Bildad in 8:13–15; compare 18:14–15.

Like the hut a watchman makes.

[19] He lies down wealthy but it will not persist;[18]
He will open his eyes—and be (wealthy) no more.[19]

[20–21] Terror will wash him away like water;[20]
A whirlwind at night will steal him away.
An east wind will lift him and blow,
Sweeping him far from his home.[21]

[22] He[22] shoots at him without sparing (an arrow);[23]
And he[24] flees in flight from his hand.

[23] People[25] clap their hands at him,
And hiss at him wherever they are."[26]

---

18. Reading *yosip* "he adds" for *ye'asep* "he is gathered" with support of the Greek and Syriac translations. For the verb *hosip* spelled with *aleph*, see for example 1 Samuel 18:20.

19. Compare Zophar in 20:7–9.

20. Compare Zophar in 20:28 and Eliphaz in 22:11. For the image, compare Hosea 5:10. The verb has the sense of "wash away" in Aramaic.

21. Compare Bildad in 18:14.

22. God. This verse alludes to Zophar's image of the wicked fleeing the weapons of the deity in 20:24–25. Only in that context can the laconic language of the verse be understood (Kahana).

23. For the context and usages, see Jeremiah 50:14.

24. The wicked.

25. Singular in the Hebrew: "one claps one's hands . . ."

26. Clapping and hissing are gestures a spectator makes when seeing the abject; see Lamentations 2:15. Job apparently alludes to Bildad's description of people's reactions to the wicked's downfall in 18:20.

JOB'S CLOSING DISCOURSE
(29:1–31:40)

Job, in his last and lengthy response to his companions, recalls his life before disasters struck. He was blessed by God and honored by people. He prides himself on his acts on behalf of others, which in a just world would have brought him good and not suffering. In this extended reverie Job reveals that he had served his community, and wayfarers as well, as a magistrate, a purveyor of justice. Accordingly, by marking Job with a stigma, the deity has not only done Job a terrible injustice, but also prevented him from providing justice to others. In order to draw the deity into a lawsuit, wherein he would explain to Job the reasons for his afflictions, Job makes an oath of innocence (Dick), a genre best known from the Egyptian Book of the Dead, in which he swears he did not perform any of the possible misdeeds that could warrant his severe punishments. If in a lawsuit one litigant swears to innocence, the onus shifts to the other party to establish his rival's guilt. Job seeks to compel the deity to respond to his lawsuit and reveal the putative charges against him.

Several verses and stanzas, especially in the latter half of this discourse, seem out of sequence. Although some interpreters seek to impose a more logical order, Job's rhetorical wavering may be meant to reflect his excited state of mind.

[**29**:1] Job again took up his discourse and he said:

[2–3] If only I could be as in months of yore,
In the days Eloah would watch over me.
When his lamp would shine over my head,
When I could walk by its light in the dark.

[4–6] Just as I'd been in my earlier[1] days,
When my tent stood under Eloah's bond;[2]
When Shaddai was still with me,
And my servants all around me;
When he would wash my feet in cream,[3]
When the Rock[4] would pour over me streams of oil.

[7–11] When I would go out to the city gate,[5]
Take my seat in the public square—
Young men would see me and withdraw,[6]
And the old would rise and stand;
Princes would hold back their words,
Placing a hand over their mouths;[7]
Leaders would stifle their voices,[8]
Their tongues clinging to their palates.

---

1. Compare Akkadian *harāpu* "to be early."
2. For this usage of *sod*, see especially Psalm 25:14.
3. Reading *hem'a* "whey, butter" for *hema* "venom, rage"; so several versions; compare for example Deuteronomy 32:13–14, to which Job alludes here.
4. For this epithet of the deity, see for example Deuteronomy 32:4, 18, 31.
5. See the comment at 5:4.
6. Compare the usage "holding back, withdrawn" in 1 Samuel 10:22.
7. Compare 21:5. The gesture indicates keeping silent in order to listen.
8. More literally, "the voices of leaders would be suppressed," the same verb rendered "withdraw" in verse 8 above.

When an ear would hear me, it would affirm;
And when an eye would see me, it would attest.

[12–13] When I would rescue the needy crying out,
And the orphan with no one to help him;[9]
When I'd receive the vagabond's blessing.
And bring joy to the heart of the widow;

[14–16] I clothed myself in the right, and it clothed me,
Justice (clothed me)[10] like a robe and a headdress.
Eyes was I to the blind,
And legs I was to the lame.
I was the patron of the poor;
And pursued the complaint of the stranger.

[17] I would break the fangs of the depraved,
And cast the prey out of his teeth.[11]

[18–20] So I thought, "I'll expire with my brood intact,[12]
And I'll multiply days like the sand![13]
My stock will be flush with water,
And dew will abide on my foliage![14]

---

9. This verse together with 29:16 below allude to Psalm 72:12–14, which describe a righteous king.

10. In the Bible and in Mesopotamian literature one speaks of being clothed by a curse (see Psalm 109:17–19). Here again Job inverts a literary convention.

11. For the figure of the wicked as a predator, see 4:10–11.

12. Literally, "in my nest (of fledglings)"; compare Deuteronomy 32:11; Isaiah 16:2.

13. Compare for example Genesis 32:13; Isaiah 48:19. Rabbinic midrash interprets "like the phoenix."

14. For the arboreal imagery and some of the language, see 14:7–9 and compare 18:16. Job sees himself as the righteous in Bildad's scenario (chapter 8).

My property[15] will be restored,[16]
And the bow in my hand replaced!"

[21–23] To me people listened, and they waited,
They kept still, as I offered my counsel.
Once I had spoken, they had nothing to add;
My speech fell on them like the rain.[17]
They would wait for my rainfall,
Their mouths open wide to catch it.[18]

[24–25] If I smiled their way, they would not swerve;[19]
If I lit up my face, they fulfilled (every word).[20]
I would choose their path and sit at their head;
I'd be poised like the king in an army—
Wherever I'd lead them, they'd camp.[21]

[30:1] But now they laugh at me—
Young men years younger than I,
Whose fathers I so detested,
I would not place them with my herding dogs!

[2–4] What need have I of their arms' strength?
Because of them the harvest[22] is lost!

---

15. For *kabod* in this sense, see for example Genesis 31:1; Isaiah 10:3.
16. Literally, "new."
17. More literally, "my word distilled upon them"; compare Deuteronomy 32:2.
18. More literally, "And their mouths they opened to the later rain."
19. For this sense, literally "to turn right," see Isaiah 30:21 and compare Job 39:24.
20. Literally, "they did not cause (the word) to fall down." For the full biblical expression, see for example 1 Samuel 3:19.
21. Reading *'obilem yaḥanu* for the received text's *'abelim yenaḥem* "mourners he comforts," which is entirely inapt. For a similar use of the verb *hobil*, see Jeremiah 31:8.
22. See the comment at 5:26.

Who in times of want and severe famine
Abscond to the desert—
To the dark,[23] the bleak, and the barren.
Who pluck the mallow bush flower,[24]
And the root of the broom-bush for food.[25]

[5] As they're driven from town,[26]
People holler as at thieves.

[6–8] To dwell[27] in the clefts of streams,
In the hollows of ground and stones.[28]
They bray among the shrubs,
They huddle at the thorn-bush.
Sons of fools and nobodies,
They're estranged[29] from the land.

[9–10] But now[30] I'm the butt of their jingles,
I've become to them a byword.[31]
They abhor me and distance themselves;
They spare no spit from my face.

---

23. For this usage, see Genesis 31:42.
24. More literally, "Who pluck the mallow on the bush."
25. These are eaten by Bedouin in desperate times (Bailey, 53–54). The verses Isaiah 47:14 and Psalm 120:4 suggest the root was burned to keep warm, in which case vocalize *lehummam* "to warm themselves" instead of *lahmam* "their food."
26. Compare *goy* in Zephaniah 2:14, synonymous with "land" or "field." In Phoenician the term indicates a community.
27. Referring back to "they abscond" in verse 3.
28. That is, in caves.
29. Reading *nikkeru* for *nikke'u* "they were smitten" or "brought low," neither of which provides the generally anticipated sense of "expelled." For *nikker* "to alienate, transfer, remove," see 1 Samuel 23:7 and the Akkadian cognate.
30. Referring back to the disrespectful youths above.
31. Compare Job 17:6; Psalm 69:12–13.

[11–14] They loosen my reins[32] and my bridle;[33]
And throw the bit off their mouths;[34]
They break the lead off their noses;[35]
They rise up and let loose their legs,[36]
And mount against me paths of destruction;
They've wrecked[37] my road, increasing my ruin,
And none can restrain[38] them.
They advance like a wide burst of water,[39]
They overrun the barren tract.

[15] Terror's been turned against me;
Blowing[40] my stature away like the wind;
My prestige[41] dissipates like a cloud.

[16–18] And now my spirit is emptied;[42]
Days of affliction take hold of me;
At night it[43] gnaws on my limbs,

---

32. The rope by which I would restrain them; reading *yitri* with the tradition. The youths are likened to a once-domesticated animal now turned wild.

33. For the verb "and they abused me" I read "my bridle" in view of Arabic *'inan* with that meaning. Recall that the poet loves synonyms.

34. Reading *mi-pihem* "from their mouths" for *mi-panai* "from my face"; compare the Syriac.

35. More literally, "My nose ring is broken off them." For the very perplexing Hebrew I read (after Ginsberg), redividing but barely changing the letters: *'aleimo napor haḥi*. The Hebrew as it stands means: "On the right a punk arise (plural)."

36. Reading *regel yeshalleḥu* for "my leg they released."

37. A pseudo-Aramaic form of Hebrew *natats*.

38. A pseudo-Aramaic form of Hebrew *'atsar*. The Arabic cognate has the sense of reining in a horse (Kister).

39. For the image, compare 2 Samuel 5:20.

40. Literally, "chasing."

41. Derived from *shoa'* "noble" (Isaiah 32:5).

42. More literally, "poured out."

43. The affliction.

So my sinews cannot rest.
It takes all my strength to change clothing;
It constrains like the neck of my tunic.

[19] It's thrown me down to the clay,
Making me seem like dust and ashes.[44]

[20–22] I cry out to you, but you do not answer;
I stand, and you just look at me.
You have turned cruel against me;
With your brute power[45] you obstruct me.[46]
You lift me to be carried off by the wind,[47]
And you sweep me away[48] in a tempest.[49]

[23] I know you'll return me to Death,[50]
To the meeting house of all who've lived.

Job's oath of innocence begins here, intermittently.

[24–25] If a poor man[51] would extend me his hand,

---

44. "Dust and ashes" is a figure for abjection; see Genesis 18:27 and compare Job 42:6.
45. Literally, "the power of your hand."
46. The verb "obstruct" is related to the name of the Satan (see comment on 1:6).
47. More literally, "you lift me to the wind and mount me upon it"; compare Psalm 18:11.
48. For this usage, compare Nahum 2:7; Psalm 65:11.
49. Reading the received text's t-sh-w-h as *teshu'ah* "tumult" as in Job 39:7; compare *sho'* "surge" in Psalm 89:10.
50. See at 28:22.
51. Reading *'im 'eilai 'ani* "If to me a poor-man" for *'ak lo' be'i* "But not in a ru-in-mound," which makes no sense (compare Dhorme and others). "Poor man" puns on "affliction" in verses 16 and 27.

If in time of disaster he cried out to me,[52]
I swear that I wept for the wretched,[53]
My spirit was pained by the needy.

[26–28] For I hoped for good, but there came bad;
I expected light, but there came darkness,
My insides roil and can't be still;
I've been greeted by days of affliction.
I walk in gloom without a sun;
In the assembly I stand and cry out.

[29–31] I've been brother to the jackal,
And companion to the ostrich;[54]
My skin has blackened off me,
And my body is charred from the heat.
My harp's been replaced by[55] wailing,
And my flute—by the voice of keeners.[56]

[**31:1**] I made a pact with my eyes,
Never to look at a maiden.

[2–4] For what is the lot from Eloah on high,
And what the portion from Shaddai above?
It's disaster for the villain,

---

52. Reading . . . *'eilai shiwa'* "to me he cried out" for *lahen shua'* "to/for them (feminine) noble," which makes no sense.
53. Literally, "the hard of day."
54. Literally, "daughters of the desert."
55. Literally, "has become."
56. Recall Job's having become the "butt of jingles" (30:9 above).

Misfortune[57] for wrongdoers.
He sees the paths (I take),
And counts my every step.

[5] I've never accompanied falsity;
My foot's never rushed toward deceit.

[6] Let him weigh me on scales of justice,
Let Eloah know how whole I am.[58]

[7–8] If my step has ever strayed from the path;
If my heart has ever followed my eyes;
If any blemish[59] has clung to my hands;
Then may I sow (my field) and another man eat (it);
And may my crops[60] be uprooted!

[9–10] If my heart has been lured to (a married) woman;
If I've ever lain in wait at my neighbor's door;[61]
Then may my wife grind[62] for another man;
And may other men crouch over her.

[11–12] For that is an unseemly act;[63]

---

57. Vocalize *nokar* for *neker*, as in Obadiah 1:12.

58. More literally, "my wholeness," my integrity; see on 1:2.

59. Reading with the Eastern Masoretic tradition; and compare Daniel 1:4. A blemish spoils the wholeness of the body, metaphorically the integrity of the person; compare Isaiah 1:6.

60. For the literal use of the term, figuratively "progeny," see for example Isaiah 34:1; 42:5.

61. In order to fornicate with his wife; compare Proverbs 7:6–22.

62. An apparent sexual innuendo (so the Talmud); see the following line.

63. The term is associated with fornication, for example in Leviticus 18:17; 20:14.

It is even a criminal offense.
It's[64] a fire that consumes all the way to Abaddon;[65]
One that would burn[66] all my produce.

[13–14] If I've ever dismissed my man-servant's claim,
Or my woman-servant's, in disputing with me—
What would I do should El rise (to judge)?[67]
If he'd call me to account—how could I answer him?

[15] Did my maker not make him in the belly like me?
Did he not fashion him the same in the womb?

[16–18] If I've ever thwarted a poor man's desires;
Or the eyes of a widow left pining;[68]
Or ate my loaf by myself,
So an orphan could not eat of it—
For since I was a boy I have reared him[69] like a father;
And her[70] I have guided since (I left) my mother's womb—[71]

[19–21] If I ever saw a vagabond with nothing to wear;
Or the needy with nothing to cover him;
If his loins did not bless me,
As he warmed in the fleece of my lambs;

---

64. The fornication; compare Proverbs 6:27–29.
65. See at 28:23.
66. Reading *tisrop* for *tesharesh* "it would uproot" (contaminated by 31:8).
67. Compare 19:25.
68. Job counters the charges Eliphaz imagined in 22:7, 9.
69. Literally, "he (the orphan) has grown up with me as his father."
70. The widow.
71. Hyperbole.

If I ever raised my hand to the fatherless
For I sighted support in the town-gate;[72]

[22–23] May the shoulder-blade fall from my shoulder,
And my arm break off at the socket!
For disaster from El is dread to me;
I cannot withstand[73] his grandeur.

[24–25] If I ever made gold my reliance,
And called pure gold "my security!"[74]
If I ever rejoiced in the size of my wealth,
That my hand had attained so much;

[26–28] If I ever looked at the light as it shone,[75]
Or the moon as it moved so nobly;[76]
If my heart was secretly lured,
So my mouth kissed my hand—[77]
That too is a criminal offense,
For denying the deity[78] above (them).[79]

[29–30] If I ever rejoiced at my enemy's ruin,
And exulted when evil befell him;

---

72. The town gate was the site of official transactions; see above at 5:2. Job never abused the powerless, even though he could get away with it.
73. One should probably read 'ahil for 'ukal; compare Jeremiah 10:10. For the sentiment, compare Job 13:11.
74. Job responds to Eliphaz's accusation in 22:24–25.
75. Apparently the light of the stars; the language alludes to Isaiah 13:10.
76. If I engaged in pagan worship.
77. A gesture of adoration; see 1 Kings 19:18 and probably Genesis 41:40.
78. Literally, "El."
79. So for example Ibn Ezra.

If I ever allowed my palate to sin,
And invoked a curse on his life;[80]

[31] If the men of my town[81] ever said,
"If we could only get our fill of his flesh!"[82]

[32] The stranger never spent a night outdoors;
I would open my doors to the wayfarer.[83]

[33–34] If I ever like Adam[84] covered my sins,
Burying my crimes in my bosom—
Intimidated by the town mob,
Frightened by the contempt of the clans,[85]
Halting, not leaving the house.[86]

[35–37] If only I had a hearing-judge![87]
Here is my mark—let Shaddai respond!
And let my rival write his indictment!
I swear I would carry it on my shoulder;
I would wear it like a crown.

---

80. Compare Job in 27:6–7.
81. More literally, "my tent."
82. See on 19:22. The if-clauses of the oaths are not completed by then-clauses in this section. It is understood that Job invokes a curse upon himself for any transgression he had actually committed.
83. One should probably revocalize 'oreaḥ (see Jeremiah 14:8).
84. So the Aramaic translation; Kahana. Compare Adam's attempts to suppress his culpability in Genesis 3:9–12.
85. Literally, "The contempt of the clans frightens me."
86. Literally, "And I halt and do not go out the entrance."
87. See Judges 11:10.

I would declare the number of my steps;[88]
And like a prince would engage him.[89]

[38–40] If ever my land has complained of me,
If ever its furrows cried out;
If ever I ate its yield without payment,[90]
And caused its owner chagrin;[91]
Let thorns grow instead of wheat,
And stinkweed instead of barley!

Completed are the words of Job.

---

88. That is, give a complete accounting.

89. "Like a prince" puns on "I would declare." More literally, "I would approach him" (in litigation). A double entendre: "I would do battle like a commander." This belligerent tone may be what provokes the belligerent response of the deity in 38:1–3.

90. Literally, "without silver."

91. See at 11:20.

ELIHU'S FIRST DISCOURSE
(32:1–33:33)

Unexpectedly, a fourth companion of Job, Elihu, insists on having his say. He is neither introduced earlier nor mentioned at the end of the book with the other three companions. These facts, together with subtle differences in language and style (for example, he addresses Job by name), lead most modern scholars to regard the four consecutive discourses of Elihu (chapters 32–37 plus 28) as a later addition to the book. The motive for inserting Elihu into this point in the dialogues, just preceding the deity's speeches (chapters 38–41), is apparent. The divine discourses dwell on God's power and majesty, not on his justice or concern for humanity—which are the elements Job has been seeking. Elihu anticipates the themes of the deity's response but crucially adds the dimensions of divine concern for humanity and morality. He provides an answer to Job: although God's ways are largely impenetrable, he sometimes induces suffering as a form of character building and discipline (compare Eliphaz in 5:17–18).

As an integral part of the present book of Job, the Elihu discourses are ironic. Meant to educate Job and enrich the deity's presentation, Elihu's bombast and sense of self-importance have an almost ludicrous effect; and the speeches by God can be understood to contradict, rather than affirm, Elihu's moral theology. God's self-representation supersedes Elihu's pretentious at-tempt to explain divine behavior.

Elihu's avowed purpose is to refute Job's arguments; in the course of his polemic he often quotes or paraphrases Job. In this first discourse Elihu justi-fies his intrusion into the dialogue and then elaborates some ways the deity manifests providential care for human beings. The discourse begins with a brief prose narrative setting the scene. Once Elihu begins speaking (in 32.6), his speech is in verse, like all the other speeches.

[**32:1**] These three men ceased responding to Job since in his own eyes he was right and just.[1]

[2–5] Elihu[2] son of Berak-El[3] the Buzite,[4] of the family of Ram,[5]
    became angry at Job;
he became angry (at him) for justifying himself before Elohim.
And at his three companions he became angry for their not finding
    a (proper) response;
they made Elohim[6] (appear to) be in the wrong.

---

1. Compare Proverbs 16:1.

2. The name means "He (or YHWH—the name of Israel's God) is God"; unlike the names of the three older companions, this name appears to be Israelite (for example 1 Samuel 1:1).

3. The name means "El (or God) Blesses"; the name is not otherwise known in the Bible.

4. Buz is the name of Uts's brother in Genesis 22:21 and a place in Edom/North Arabia in Jeremiah 25:23.

5. Ram is an Israelite name (Ruth 4:19 and elsewhere), although some from ancient to modern times identify it with Aram.

6. The received Hebrew text has "Job," not "Elohim," here; but rabbinic tradition (for example Midrash Tanḥuma; compare Rashi, Ibn Ezra, and others) identifies this as a late scribal correction intended to save the deity's honor.

So Elihu waited out Job's words,[7] since they[8] were much older than
    he in years.[9]
When Elihu saw there was no (proper) response in the mouths of
    these three men, he became angry.

[6–10] Up spoke Elihu son of Berak-El the Buzite and he said:

Young am I in years[10]
Whereas you are elderly.[11]
That's why I was too timid and afraid
To express my discourse[12] to you.
I thought, (the many of) days should speak,
The many in years should make wisdom known.[13]
There is however a spirit within mortals;
Shaddai's breath gives them understanding.
It is not the many (of years) who get wisdom,
Nor the old who understand custom.[14]
That's why I say: "Listen to me!
I too will express my discourse."

[11–12] I have been abiding your speeches,

---

7. The Hebrew here is clumsy.

8. The three companions—Eliphaz, Bildad, and Zophar.

9. Literally, "days."

10. Literally, "days."

11. Elihu is here addressing the companions, not Job.

12. The term *dea'/ de'ah* (and sometimes *da'at*) is derived from the verb *da'a* "to speak" (see Proverbs 24:14), not *yada'* "to know," as is commonly thought. The phrase "to express discourse" is unique to Elihu.

13. "Make known" echoes "my discourse." Elihu may be invoking a traditional saying (Fontaine).

14. The term *mishpat*, most often "judgment, justice," can also denote "regimen, custom, manner" (for example Genesis 40:13; 2 Samuel 27:11; 2 Kings 17:33).

Giving ear to your explanations—[15]
While you examined[16] (Job's) words.
I have observed your discourse,[17]
And I find: not one of you proves Job wrong;
Not one answers his assertions.

[13–14] Perhaps you'll say, "We've found a wise course:
El, not a man, will defeat[18] him."
But had he put his case to me,[19]
I would not respond with your assertions.

[15–16] Confounded,[20] they[21] spoke up no more;
They were at a loss for words.[22]
I abided till they were no more speaking;
They stopped and responded no more.

[17–20] I will have my own part spoken;
I too will express my discourse.
For I am filled with words;
Bloated by the wind in my belly.
My belly, you see, is like unopened wine;

---

15. "Your understandings."
16. See Proverbs 18:17: "The righteous may be first in his lawsuit, but then comes his counterpart and cross-examines him."
17. Reading we-de'ikem for we-'adekem "at you."
18. Literally, "drive him off."
19. Reading lu' "if, would" for the received lo' "not" (so Masnuth and some moderns). Compare the comment on 9:33.
20. For this usage, see Isaiah 37:27.
21. The three older companions. In this verse and the next Elihu is addressing an audience, as in theater.
22. Literally, "words moved away from them" or "they moved words away from themselves."

And like a new wineskin will burst.
I must speak to enjoy relief;
I must open my lips and speak up.

[21–22] Let me show favor to no one;[23]
Nor defer to a gentleman's title.[24]
If I'd[25] favor a man for his title,[26]
Then my creator would carry me off.

[**33**:1–4] But you, Job, pray hear my words;
To all that I speak give your ear!
You see I have opened my mouth;
My tongue speaks from inside my palate.[27]
All that I say is (from) my upright heart,
The speech of my lips—honest discourse.[28]
The spirit of El has created me;
The breath of Shaddai invigorates me.

[5–7] If you are able—answer me!
Set yourself before me—make your case!
Before El I am just like you;
I too have been pinched from clay.[29]

---

23. Contrary to the older companions, according to Job (13:8).
24. For this usage, see Isaiah 44:5; 45:4.
25. The vocalization *lu'* for *lo'* "not" is based on the formula "if . . . then . . ." (*lu* . . . *kim'at*); see Psalm 94:17.
26. More literally, "If would favor whom I would title."
27. "Palate" is apparently a metonym for "mouth."
28. Literally, "The discourse of my lips they speak sincerely" (compare Kahana).
29. "To pinch off clay" is a figure for creating a human in the ancient Semitic world; compare 10:9.

See, my awesome mien will not terrify you;
My pressure will not feel heavy to you.[30]

[8–11] Yet you have said in my ears;
These words in your voice I have heard:
"Pure am I, without transgression;
I am innocent, I've done no crime![31]
But he[32] finds pretexts[33] against me;
He regards me as his enemy.[34]
He's marked my feet with lime;
Watching my every step."[35]

[12–13] Where you are not right I will answer you;
For Eloah is greater than mortals.
Why do you complain against him,
That he'll answer no one's[36] charges?

[14–17] For one time El will speak (and be heard),
But a second time he[37] will not see it.[38]
In a dream, a vision in the night,

---

30. Elihu alludes to Job's reasons for fearing a confrontation with the deity in 13:21. The term for "force, pressure" here puns on "your hand" there.

31. Elihu paraphrases Zophar's pseudo-quotation of Job in 11:4.

32. God.

33. Reading to'anot for ten'uot "depredations" (with the ancient Syriac, Rashi, and others); compare for example Judges 14:4; 2 Kings 5:7

34. Quoting Job in 13:24; compare 19:11.

35. Quoting Job in 13:27.

36. Literally, "will not answer his (a human's) words (legal charges)."

37. A human.

38. Will not realize it. The unrecognized revelation is in a nocturnal vision. Elihu turns Job's complaint (4:12–21) into a positive.

When slumber falls upon people,[39]
When they're lying down to sleep,[40]
Then does he open people's ears,[41]
Frightening them[42] with (his) discipline;[43]
To turn one away from one's misdeeds
And remove[44] the pride[45] from a man.

[18–22] He spares his life from the pit,[46]
His vigor from crossing the channel.[47]
For he's reproved when he's lying in pain,
And his limbs in a constant tremor.[48]
His throat treats his bread as rotten;
His gullet most delectable food.[49]
His flesh wastes away out of sight;
His never seen bones are laid bare.[50]
His life-force approaches the pit,
And his vigor the locus of death.[51]

---

39. A quotation from the report (of Job) in 4:13.

40. Literally, "when sleep falls upon the place-of-lying-down."

41. A biblical expression for revealing a secret.

42. Reading *yeḥittem* for *yaḥtom* "he seals."

43. The means by which he will educate them. For the term see also 36:10 and compare 5:17 (Eliphaz).

44. Literally, "cover."

45. Aramaic; compare Daniel 4:34.

46. The grave.

47. See Ezekiel 31:5; Nehemiah 3:15. Crossing the channel is apparently an image of dying, as in Mesopotamia (the River Hubur) and Greece (the River Styx). See also 36:12.

48. For *rob* "shivers, tremor," see at 4:3.

49. His gullet treats the most desirable food as rotten.

50. Compare 19:20.

51. One should probably vocalize *memotim* as in Jeremiah 16:4 and Ezekiel 28:8 (Held, "Pits and Pitfalls").

[23–24] But if he has a guardian-angel,
Just one champion[52] out of a thousand,
To declare a person upright,
He[53] will appeal (to El), saying:
"I will redeem him[54] from entering the pit;
I have found the ransom funds."

[25–26] His flesh then grows plumper[55] than a child's;
It returns to the days of his youth.
He'll entreat Eloah, who'll accept him;
Show him in gladness[56] his face;
Return the mortal his rightful status.

[27–28] He'll return[57] then to the men[58] and announce:
"I have sinned! I've accused the Upright[59] of crime;
And it was not worth my while.
He's redeemed me[60] from entering the pit;
So my life can bask in the light."

---

52. An "intercessor."
53. The angel.
54. Reading 'epdehu for the peculiar form pedaʿehu "redeem him!" with an ʿayin instead of an aleph. For the sequence and verb form, see Psalm 49:8.
55. The r at the head of the verb is an apparent dittograph from the preceding word.
56. For the sense of "gladness," see the parallel to śimḥa in 3:21.
57. Reading yashub for yashor, an anomalous form of "he'll sing"—a likely contamination from yashar "upright" in the next line. For the usage, compare Hosea 5:15.
58. To Job, these are his three companions, referred to above as the three "men" (32:1, 5).
59. An epithet of the deity; see Deuteronomy 32:4; Psalms 25:8; 92:16; compare Psalm 119:137. The same term used to indicate Job's character: "straight (of path)" (1:1, 8; 2:3).
60. Reading the Ketib (written traditional text) here and in the following line.

[29–30] These things El performs
Two or three times for a man:[61]
Returning his life from the pit,
To bask in the light of the living.

[31–33] Pay heed now, Job, hear me!
Keep silent now and I will speak![62]
If you have words, then answer me!
Speak, for I want to acquit you!
But if you have none, then hear me!
Keep silent and I'll teach you wisdom!

---

61. In the course of a life.
62. Elihu parodies Job's address to his companions in 13:13.

ELIHU'S SECOND DISCOURSE
(34:1–37)

Elihu addresses the group of companions, seeking empathy for his derision of Job, who has deigned to challenge the dogma of divine justice. He then asserts that God is always and only just, as he appeals to the group, to Job individually, and again to the group. Elihu takes issue with Job's arguments in chapters 21 and 24 in particular. In the end he presses Job to desist from asking the deity for explanations and to drop his lawsuit. (Elihu's redundancies so irritated the ancient Greek translator that he omitted many repetitious lines.)

[**34:1**] Up spoke Elihu and he said:

[2–4] Hear my words, O men of wisdom!
Give ear to me, O men of knowledge!
"For an ear tests words
As the palate tastes food."[1]

---

1. For "taste" as a metaphor of reason, see the comment on 6:6. For *le'ekol* "to eat" read *lo 'okel* on the basis of 12:11, where the same traditional saying is quoted. So several ancient versions.

Let us examine[2] the charges,
So together we can find what's correct.[3]

[5–6] For Job has said, "I'm in the right;
But El's set aside my charges.[4]
For the charges against me I'm pained;[5]
Although I've not sinned, my 'arrow'[6] is fatal."

[7–9] What man like Job
Drinks scorn like water;[7]
And keeps company with workers of evil,
Traveling with wicked men?![8]
For he's said: "A man does not benefit
When he pleases Elohim."[9]

[10–11] And so, men of mind,[10]
Listen to me!
Wickedness—far be it[11] from El!
Far be wrongdoing from Shaddai!
For he pays a person his (fair) wage;
Provides in line with one's conduct.

---

2. In Aramaic synonymous with *baḥan* "test" in the preceding verse.
3. Literally, "good"; but *tob* has the basic meaning of "sweet." Thus "sweet taste" (verse 3) suggests "reasonable."
4. Quoting Job in 27:2.
5. Reading *'ekʾab* for *'akazzeb* "I lie, disappoint," which makes no sense here. Compare Jeremiah 15:18.
6. Divine affliction; see 6:4.
7. Elihu turns Job's image in 6:4 against him. He is paraphrasing Eliphaz's parody of the spirit in 15:16.
8. Compare the scene described in Proverbs 1:10–19.
9. Job has not said precisely this; but compare Malachi 3:14.
10. Literally, "heart"; compare 12:3.
11. Elihu echoes or mimics Job's "God forbid" in 27:5.

[12-13] In truth, El does not do evil;
Shaddai does not corrupt justice.[12]
Who gives him charge of the land?
Puts the whole earth in his hands?[13]

[14-15] If he returns[14] its spirit to him,
And gathers its breath to himself,
All that is flesh will expire,
And the human returns to the dust.

[16] If you've understanding, pray hear this![15]
Pray give ear to the gist[16] of my words!

[17-20] Would a hater of justice bind (wounds)?[17]
Would you condemn the Eminently Righteous—[18]
Who would call[19] a king worthless,
(Who would call) nobles wicked;
Who would show no favor to officers;
Nor treat[20] magnates better than poor folk—
For they all are the work of his hands?
In an instant they can die,

---

12. Elihu answers Bildad's rhetorical question in 8:3.
13. Literally, "Who has imposed (on him) the entire earth?"
14. Reading *yashib* for *yasim* "he places," with the eastern Masoretic tradition. Compare Psalm 104:29. The word *libbo* "his heart" in the received text was apparently added secondarily to furnish an object to "he places."
15. The singular indicates Elihu is now addressing Job.
16. The word "voice" (*qol*) can by metonymy indicate a message (for example Leviticus 5:1).
17. Compare 5:18.
18. The deity. Compare God's words in 40:8.
19. Revocalizing *ha'amor* "calling" as *ha'omer* in line with some ancient versions. The deity gives equal justice to all.
20. Literally, "recognize"; a rare usage of the *Pi'el* form in this sense (so BDB).

In dead of night[21] they can pass;[22]
They expire like a moth;[23]
They perish[24] by no (human) hand.

[21–22] For his eyes are (trained) on the ways of a man;
And all of his steps he sees.[25]
There is no darkness or deathly-shade
Where workers of evil can hide.[26]

[23] Thus a man should no more make a case,[27]
To enter a lawsuit with El.

[24–27] He smashes the eminent without limit;
And installs others in their stead.
He surely knows their activities;
He turns over the night and they're crushed![28]
He strikes them down where the wicked stand,
In a place where all can see;
Because they strayed from behind him,
And none of his ways did they learn:

---

21. Perhaps an allusion to the tenth plague in Egypt (Exodus 12:29).

22. The verse is by many modern accounts in disorder; I read the verb phrase "they pass" at the end of this line, not the next.

23. Reading *yigwe'u 'im 'ash* for *yego'ashu 'am* "the people are in turmoil," which is inapt; it is the death of the powerful that is relevant. For the image, compare Psalm 39:12.

24. Reading *yasuru* for *we-yasiru* "they remove." The word *'abbir* "bull, potentate" is a dittography of *(lo)' beyad* "not by hand." The scribe forgot to write the *l*, realized his mistake, and recopied, without erasing the mistake (see above at 22:8).

25. Compare Job in 31:4. Job has found divine surveillance to be hostile; compare 14:16.

26. Contra Job's account in 24:14–17.

27. For this expression, see at 23:6.

28. The discourse picks up the argument of verses 21–22 above. Elihu alludes to the wording of Job, quoting the spirit, in 4:19. Compare the image used by the deity in 38:13–15.

[28-29] To bring to him the poor man's cry;
So he can hear the cry of the indigent.
When he calms[29] (it) down,
Who would stir (it) up?[30]
When he hides his face,
Who could perceive it?

He looks[31] over people and nations;
[30] So an impudent man does not reign—
Not one who entraps his people.[32]

[31-32] Thus to Eloah you must say:[33]
"I will bear (the yoke), I will not break (it).[34]
What I cannot see myself, you must teach me.
If I have done an injustice, I will do so no more."

[33] Should he reward you as you reckon,[35]
Though you are "fed up"?[36]
(Saying,)[37] "You should choose, not I.
Whatever you think—speak!"

---

29. More literally, "quiets."
30. The verb *hirshia*, ordinarily "to act wickedly," in Job has the sense of *hir'ish* "to cause noise" (Ibn Ezra, Masnuth); see at 3:17.
31. The line "over people and nation together" is a fragment. For *yahad* "together" I read, with Ehrlich, *yahaz* "he looks" (short form); compare the short form *'ahaz* "I look" in 23:9.
32. In sin; compare for example Exodus 23:33; 34:12. Literally, "one of the traps of the people." This verse continues the theme of verses 24-27.
33. Slightly redividing the words (with some moderns): *'el 'eloah 'emor* for "to El be said," which is also ungrammatical.
34. The object of the verbs is apparently the "yoke" (*'ol*) of the deity; see Lamentations 3:27 and Isaiah 10:27, respectively (so Hakham).
35. Literally, "from what is with you"; for a similar usage, see 10:13.
36. Elihu alludes to Job in 7:16.
37. Compare Ehrlich, Hakham.

[34–35] Men of mind[38] will tell me,
Any wise man who hears me (will):
"Job speaks not from knowledge;
His words have no insight."

[36–37] Would that Job be tested forever,
The way men of evil are answered![39]
For he keeps adding to his sin;
Among us his crime is unbounded;[40]
And he multiplies[41] words against El.

---

38. See note 10 above.
39. Literally, "through answers against men of iniquity."
40. For sapak "be abundant," see Isaiah 2:6.
41. The verb (yireb) puns on the term for bringing legal charges (rib).

ELIHU'S THIRD DISCOURSE
(35:1–16)

Elihu seeks to correct some of Job's misguided reactions. A person's good or bad behavior affects other people, not the deity. If the deity does not respond to supplication, it is not from divine indifference but from disdain toward the suppliant. Accordingly, God is not ignoring Job's complaint; Job needs to wait more patiently.

[**35:1**] Up spoke Elihu and he said:

[2–3] Is this why you planned your lawsuit:
You thought, "I am more just than God!"
When you asked, what's the profit to you"
"How do I gain from not sinning?"[1]

[4] I will put words back to you—
And your companions as well.

---

1. Elihu is inferring that Job said this because Eliphaz appears to reject such a claim in 22:2–3; see the comment there.

[5–7] Look up at the heavens and observe;
See how the sky is much higher than you!
If you've sinned, what can you do to him?[2]
As your crimes multiply, what do you do for him?
If you are just, what do you give him?
What does he get from your hand?

[8] When you're wicked, it affects your fellow man;
And when you're just, it affects another person.

[9–10] When the many oppress,[3] people cry out;
When the many wield power,[4] they call for aid.
They[5] do not say, "Where is Eloah my Maker,[6]
The Grantor of Strength[7] in the night?"

[11] He more than wild beasts instructs us;
More than birds of the sky makes us wise.[8]

[12] When[9] they cry out, and he does not answer—
It's because of the bad people's pride.[10]

---

2. A quotation of Job in 7:20.

3. Literally, "On account of many oppressors." For the form of this word, compare Jeremiah 22:3.

4. More literally, "on account of the arm of many."

5. The Hebrew has the singular, referring back to the "man" and "person" of verse 8. The Qumran Aramaic and some other versions understand a plural here.

6. A conventional prayer formula; see for example 2 Kings 2:14.

7. Reading *zemarot* (singular: *zimra;* for example Exodus 15:2) for *zemirot* "songs." Compare Psalm 68:36: "He grants power and might."

8. Elihu is overturning Job's assertion in 12:8.

9. For the sense of "when," analogous to Arabic *thamma,* compare Micah 3:4.

10. Elihu explains that the deity's seeming indifference to some sufferers is their fault— they are too proud to ask for God's help; see verse 10. Compare Micah 3:4.

[13] For El will not hear insincerity;
Shaddai will not look at it.

[14–15] All the more to your saying,
"You do not look at it!"[11]
The matter's before him,
And you must wait.[12]
For he neither punishes[13] in anger,
Nor greatly harms[14] the sinner.[15]

[16] Yet Job widens his mouth[16] with wind;
He multiplies words without knowledge.

---

11. At his case.

12. Contra Job, who has said he cannot bear waiting for a hearing (13:15). For the unique form *teholel* read probably *titholel* "wait"; see Psalm 37:7.

13. Vocalizing *poqed* in accord with the use of the negative particle *ein* (for *ayin* "nought"). For the sense, compare Psalm 89:33.

14. Reading *yarea'* for *yada'* "know"; for the construal with the preposition *b* see for example Psalm 74:3.

15. Reading *beposhea'* (compare the ancient versions for *bappash*, which, though seemingly from the verb *push* "spread," is completely anomalous. The entire verse is problematic.

16. For the negative connotation of this phrase, see for example Psalm 22:14.

ELIHU'S FOURTH DISCOURSE
(36:1-37:24; 28:1-28)

In this lengthy final speech Elihu seeks further to disabuse Job of his mistaken notions. Contrary to Job's assertions, the deity does provide appropriate justice to the righteous and the wicked, without showing favor to the privileged. In fact, contrary to Job's mock wisdom (chapter 12), God does not simply bring down monarchs; he tries to teach them by disciplining them, in a way reminiscent of Eliphaz's lecture to Job in 5:17-18. Elihu warns Job of losing his erstwhile values. In adducing the deity's control over the rain, Elihu sets the scene for his sweeping description of divine wisdom, beyond human grasp, high in the heavens (chapter 37) and deep in the earth (chapter 28).

[**36:1**] Elihu spoke again and he said:

[2-4] Stay with me a while and I'll tell you;[1]
For Eloah has more words to say:

---

1. This line is entirely in Aramaic (so Rashi).

"I'll take up my discourse from afar;[2]
And provide my creature with justice."
My words, in truth, are no lie;[3]
You have here a man of honest intent.

[5-6] El, you see, is eminent in strength,
And does not reject the pure of heart.[4]
He does not keep the wicked in life;[5]
But fairness he gives to the meek.[6]
He does not pry justice[7] from the righteous.

[7-10] He places[8] kings on the throne,
Seating them forever up high.
But if he binds them[10] in shackles;
(If) they're caught in cords of affliction;
He reveals to them their misdeeds,

---

2. Although most understand Elihu to be speaking, the deity, not Elihu, can speak to Job "from afar." Moreover, others must interpret "my creature" (po'ali "the work [of my hands]"; see for example Psalm 90:16) as "my Maker"; but this well-attested term is nowhere else used this way.

3. Contra Job's characterization of the companions in 13:4.

4. The received Hebrew is very awkward. Elihu is clearly responding to Job's claims in 9:19, 22, and elsewhere. On the basis of Job 9:4 (Job) and 8:20 (Bildad), respectively, I read (similarly to Clines, *Job 21-37*): *hen 'ei kabbir koah/welo' rim'as bar lebab*.

5. Elihu is rebutting Job in 21:7.

6. Ordinarily "the poor"; however, the term *'aniyyim* often stands for *'anawim* "the meek," as in Psalm 9:13 (Tur-Sinai).

7. On the basis of the Greek version, read here (with several moderns) *dino* for *'ena(y)w* "his eyes." If "his eyes" is original, however, compare Psalm 34:16. This line belongs to verse 7 in the traditional text.

8. Reading *we-shat* for *we-'et* (direct object indicator, which is odd since there is no verb); see Psalm 137:11. (For another mistaken writing of *aleph* for *shin*, see Proverbs 28:18: *'ahat* "one" written for *shahat* "pit.")

9. Contrast Job in 12:17-18.

10. Reading *'asaram* for *'asurim* "they are bound"; the deity is the subject; compare the recapitulating form in verse 13.

Their growing number of crimes.
He opens their ears to (his) discipline,[11]
Saying, turn back from iniquity.

[11–14] If they pay heed and do (as he says),[12]
They will end their days in bounty,[13]
And their years in prosperity.
But if they do not pay heed,
They will cross the channel,[14]
Expiring for lack of wisdom.
For the impudent of heart will be brazen:[15]
Though bound,[16] they will not pray.
They will die at (the peak of their) youth;
Lose life among the reckless young.[17]

[15–16] He pulls the poor out of affliction,
And opens their ears[18] through distress.[19]
He draws you away[20] from adversity—
An expanse with below nothing firm;[21]
And now your table is lavishly set.[22]

---

11. See at 33:18.
12. The verb is used in its Aramaic sense; compare 34:25.
13. Echoing Job in 21:3.
14. See at 33:18.
15. Literally, "they do not put the nose," a unique idiom. Compare the phrase "to raise the horn," a figure from the realm of animals which has the sense of showing pride.
16. Literally, "although he (the deity) has bound them."
17. Literally, "their life-force (will die) among male prostitutes."
18. Informs them; see verse 10.
19. "Distress" puns on "pulls out" in the preceding line.
20. For this usage of the verb, see 2 Chronicles 18:31.
21. Compare 37:10.
22. Literally, "the top of your table is full of rich food." "Top" is apparently cognate with Ugaritic nḫt "seat."

[17] The case against the wicked you do not make;[23]
But claims against the orphan you support.[24]

[18–19] Beware[25] lest affluence draw you in;
Lest rich reward lead you astray.
Can your prestige be compared to gold?[26]
Can any of your mighty efforts?[27]

[20] Do not yearn through the night,
For the folk to rise up from their places.[28]

[21] Beware, do not turn to iniquity!
For this you've been tested[29] by affliction!

[22–26] El, you see, excels in power;
There is no master[30] like him.
Who commands him how to govern?
And who can say, "you've done wrong?"

---

23. The Hebrew makes little sense as a whole, so moderns tend to emend it heavily; meanings the Hebrew cannot bear are often proposed. I read this line (with Tur-Sinai): we-din resha'im lo' tadin, literally, "the judgment of the wicked you do not judge."

24. Reading (compare Leveque): u-mishpat yatom itmok. The line would be too short without assuming a word, such as yatom—which shares letters with the following verb—was accidentally omitted. Compare Eliphaz in 22:5–9.

25. Reading hemeh (Aramaic); for the Hebrew equivalent, see verse 21. The preceding word ki is dittography from the preceding line.

26. Reading le-betser for lo' be-tsar "not in distress" or the like.

27. For the phrase "mighty efforts" in the sense of wealth, see Proverbs 24:5. It could also mean: "Can any of your enterprises (be compared to gold)?"

28. To begin the workday? Compare Job in the first part of chapter 7. The connection of the verse to the surrounding context is unclear. Many different readings and interpretations have been offered.

29. Vocalizing boharta, the passive form of the Aramaic verb "test." The syntax is still curious.

30. A Hebraized form of Aramaic mare' (Daniel 2:47; 5:23).

Pay mind to exalt his work,
Which people have admired![31]
All humanity looks upon it;
Mortals gaze from afar.
El, you see, is more exalted than we know;
His years are a limitless number.

[27–28] For he sheds[32] drops of water,
Pours[33] rain on humanity;[34]
As the skies precipitate,
Showering all humanity.

[29–30] Who knows[35] how he spreads the clouds,[36]
Or the booming from behind them?[37]
He lays his lightning[38] over them,
And covers the floor[39] of the sea.

[31] With it he sustains[40] the nations,
Providing food in abundance.

---

31. A form of *shur*, literally, "to see, look" (so Masnuth and others).

32. The verb *gara'* connotes raining in rabbinic Hebrew.

33. Pseudo-Aramaic form of Hebrew *yatsoq*; compare Rashbam on Job 28:2.

34. Reading *le'adam* for *le'eido* "for its mist." Elihu is correcting the deity's assertion in 38:26, according to which God provides rain specifically where people do not dwell. The shared stems for "rain" and "humanity" tighten the link.

35. Reading *mi yabin* for *'im yabin* "if he understands." Compare 37:15–16.

36. Literally, "the spreads of cloud."

37. Literally, the booming of the "screen," or thicket of cloud providing a screen for the deity; compare Psalm 18:12.

38. Literally, "light"; compare 37:3, 11, 15.

39. Literally, "roots, bottom."

40. Reading *yazin* (Aramaic) for *yadin* "judge"; compare Jeremiah 5:8 and the noun *mazon* "food."

[32-33] Above the clouds[41] he stores the lightning,
Ordaining it[42] to one who is praying.[43]
His thunder[44] alerts him[45] (of it),
And the tempest[46] his cattle.

[37:1] It really makes my heart flutter,[47]
Makes it leap out of its place!

[2-5] Hear oh hear the shudder of his thunder,
The sound coming out of his mouth![48]
He flashes[49] from beneath the whole sky,
His lightning o'er the span[50] of the land.
Then he roars his thunder:
Booming in his surging voice.
He does not hold back bolts,[51]
So his voice can be heard.
El's voice thunders wondrously;[52]
He performs great things beyond our ken.

---

41. Literally, "hands, palms." A metaphor for "clouds" (Rashbam); compare 1 Kings 18:44: "Behold: a small cloud like a person's palm/hand arising from the sea."
42. For "light/lightning" as a feminine noun, see Jeremiah 13:16.
43. For this usage, see Isaiah 59:16 (so for example Rashbam, Masnuth, Meyuhhas). The same verb is used in this sense in the Qal conjugation in Job 21:15.
44. Compare for example Micah 4:9.
45. The person praying for rain.
46. Reading 'al'ola "storm" in Aramaic.
47. Literally, "At it (the lightning) my heart trembles."
48. In the ancient Near East and the Bible thunder is figured, and perhaps understood, as the voice of the storm god.
49. Reading yishrah; the verb sharah is found in this context in ancient Canaanite (Ugaritic).
50. Literally, "the wings, edges."
51. To complete the short line I read (with Budde, Dhorme) ye'aqqeb beragim "he restrains lightning-bolts," assuming the omission of three repeated letters.
52. Literally, "El thunders with his voice wondrously."

[6] He orders the snow, "Fall[53] to earth!"
And the rain, the staves of his strength.[54]

[7–8] He seals all humanity in,
Letting them know of his works.
Wild animals enter[55] their dens,
Settling down in their lairs.

[9–10] The storm winds come out of their chamber,
The chill (comes) out of the storerooms.[56]
By the breath of El ice is made;[57]
Expanses of water turn solid.

[11–13] He weighs down with moisture the clouds;
The nimbus[58] scatters his lightning;
And it[59] whirls around on all sides—
They behave in accord with his plan,
However he directs them to cover the earth[60]—
Whether to punish the land,[61]
Or to favor it he bestows them.

---

53. An Arabism and not the Hebrew or Aramaic verb "to be."
54. Reading *mattot 'uzzo*; see Ezekiel 19:11. The scribe began writing *mattot* but wrote *matar* "rain" by mistake; he then continued copying correctly. Unfortunately, a later scribe added a *resh* to *mattot,* producing an awkward text.
55. Reading *we-tabo'* for *wa-tabo'* "entered."
56. Reading *mezawim* (Psalm 144:13) for the unique term *mezarim.* For the image, see Job 38:22.
57. Literally, "he/it gives (ice)." The subject is unclear—possibly the celestial "chamber" (verse 9); many read a passive form of the verb ("the ice is given/made").
58. Reading the noun as an unbound form (not "cloud of . . .").
59. The lightning.
60. The final phrase is, more literally, "over the face of the land earthward."
61. The second instance of *'im* "whether" preceding "the land" is a scribal error.

[14] Give ear to this, Job!
Stand and contemplate
The wonders of El!

[15–17] Do you know how he enjoins them—
And lightning gleams out of his clouds?
Do you know how he spreads the clouds,
A wonder of the Wholly Knowing?[62]
(Do you know) why your garments are hot,
When the south wind is calm in the land?[63]

[18] Can you beat out[64] the sky-dome as he can—
Solid as a mirror of metal?[65]

[19–20] Tell us, how can we answer him?[66]
We're in the dark and have no (words) to offer.[67]
Will he be informed if I try to speak—
Has a man what to say when confused?[68]

[21–22] When people cannot see the sun,[69]
It's obscured[70] in the heavens,

---

62. Here an epithet of the deity. The same phrase as "(man) of honest intent" in 36:4.
63. Literally, "when the land is calm without the south wind."
64. The dome of the sky is typically figured as a beaten sheet of metal; the sky is called "the beaten plate" (*raqia'*) in Genesis 1:6 and elsewhere.
65. Mirrors were typically made of bronze (compare Exodus 38:8). Literally, "strong as a solid mirror."
66. Elihu imagines that God is asking the questions—as he does in the subsequent divine discourses.
67. Compare the full phrase at 32:14.
68. For this sense of *bala'*, see Isaiah 28:7.
69. Literally, "the Light."
70. Compare *baheret* "skin discoloration" in Leviticus 13:2, 4, etc. from a stem with the general sense of "clear, bright." The poet enjoys ironic puns.

A wind blows across and they're clear.[71]
A glow[72] emerges from the north,[73]
An aura about the awesome Eloah.

[23–24] Shaddai—we cannot reach him,[74]
Exalted in power and dominion!
Abounding in justice, he does not afflict.[75]
That is why people revere him;
The wisest of heart cannot see (him).

In the preceding passage (37:14–24), Elihu describes the uncanny marvels of the created world in the upper realm, in the sky. In the present passage (chapter 28), Elihu continues to describe a world that is beyond human comprehension, now focusing on the lower realm, the earth and, more particularly, the subterranean, which includes both the netherworld—the domain of the dead—and the sea that was believed to lie beneath the land. The passage is structured by two questions that ask, Where can (divine) wisdom be found? The question turns out to be a riddle, for the answer is not about where, but when (see verses 25–27).

Modern commentators tend to regard chapter 28, which does not comport with Job's perspectives, as an independent poem that cannot be attributed to any of the known speakers. The assumption that the poem is autonomous is highly problematic. Biblical poems do not begin with the conjunction ki, *"for, because," as this passage does. There is no antecedent to the pronoun "he" in verse 3. But more important, the motif of esoteric wisdom lying beyond human*

---

71. Literally, "it makes them (the heavens) pure/clear."
72. Reading *zohar* for *zahab* "gold."
73. Perhaps the northern lights.
74. Compare 11:7–8.
75. Does not afflict without just cause.

reach typically includes both the above and the below (see for example Job 11:7–8; Deuteronomy 30:11–13; Jeremiah 31:36; as well the Babylonian hymn to the sun god Shamash). The conclusion of this passage (28:28) echoes the conclusion of the survey of the heavenly wonders in 37:24, and it is following that passage that this one belongs.[76]

Most modern commentators and translators, in contrast to the medieval Jewish exegetes, interpret the first part of this passage to deal with human mining activity. This interpretation, though widespread, is unfounded. There is not a single term associated with excavating in the Hebrew text. And all the enumerated activities are elsewhere attributed to the deity. It is God who exposes the subterranean, not people (see the notes). Reference to precious ore that is extracted from the ground serves as a contrast to wisdom, which cannot be drawn out of any site.

The passage begins in response to the prompt in 37:23: "we cannot reach him," an allusion to 11:7–8 (Zophar), where God is said to be out of reach in both "the heights of heaven" and "deeper than Sheol."

[28:1–2] There is a site whence silver comes,
And a place for refining gold.
Iron is removed from the ground,
And copper is poured out of stone.

[3–4] He[77] puts an end to darkness,
And he probes to every extreme—
Stone, dark, and deathly-shade.[78]

---

76. So also Clines, "The Fear of the Lord"; *Job 21–37*.

77. The deity, Eloah/Shaddai, referred to in 37:22–23. The deity's prowess contrasts with the limited abilities of humanity.

78. For the deity as the one who probes the earth's depths and reveals light beneath the darkness, see for example 11:7; 12:22; 26:10; 38:19–20; Isaiah 42:16; other passages may also be compared.

He breaks open streams[79] where no one dwells,
Forgotten by travelers,
Neglected by wayfarers.[80]

[5–6] Land from which comes crystal,[81]
And below which jasper[82] (glows) like fire.
A place whose stones are sapphire,
And whose soil is gold.

[7–8] A path no vulture has known,
Never caught by the eye of a hawk.
Never trod by wild beasts,
Never walked by a lion.

[9–10] He reaches his hand down to flint-stone,
From the root overturns mountains.[83]
He breaks open channels[84] in rock,[85]
And his eye beholds everything precious.

[11] He exposes[86] the well-springs[87] of rivers,
And their[88] secrets he brings to light.

---

79. The plural suffix—*m* was omitted by haplography (preceding another *m*).
80. More literally, "(the streams are) low in people passing by."
81. Reading *'aḥlam* for *leḥem* "bread," which is inapt here; see the feminine form in Exodus 28:19; 39:12.
82. Reading *nopek* for *nehpak* "turned over"; see Ezekiel 28:13–14.
83. For this as divine activity, see 9:5 above.
84. The Hebrew (*ye'orim*) puns on "light" (*'or* in verse 11).
85. For this as divine activity, see for example Habakkuk 3:9; Psalms 74:15; 78:15; 114:8.
86. Reading *ḥasap* for *ḥibbesh* "binds up"; compare 12:22.
87. Vocalizing *mabbekei*, cognate to *nebek* in 38:16 and known in that form in Ugaritic.
88. Altering the feminine possessive suffix to suit the masculine plural reference.

[12] But where can wisdom be found,
And what is the site of understanding?

[13–14] No human knows the way there,[89]
As it cannot be found in the land of the living.
The Deep[90] says, "It is not in me,"
And Sea[91] says, "It is not with me."

[15–19] It cannot be purchased with bullion [92]
Its price can't be weighed out in silver
Nor placed on the balance with gold of Ophir,[93]
Nor with precious carnelian or sapphire.
It can't be compared to gold or quartz,
Nor exchanged for the finest of jewelry.[94]
It cannot be mentioned with coral or crystal;
For wisdom is worth[95] more than rubies.
It can't be compared with the topaz of Cush [96]
Nor poised on the balance with pure gold.

[20] But whence does wisdom come,
And what is the site of understanding?

---

89. Reading *darkah* for *'erkah* "its value" with the Greek; a contamination from verses 17 and 19.

90. The subterranean sea, often rendered "the abyss" in Genesis 1:2 and elsewhere. The Deep is the home of the Canaanite father-god and purveyor of wisdom, El.

91. Yamm in 7:12.

92. *Sagur* "solid gold" in 1 Kings 6:20–21; 7:49, 50; known also from Akkadian. The present digression on wisdom's being more valuable than jewels elaborates similar passages in Proverbs 3:14–15 and 8:10–11.

93. See at Job 22:24.

94. More literally, "jewelry of fine gold."

95. Reading *mekes* (Leviticus 27:23) for *mesnek* "leather pouch." In Job the letter *sin* often serves instead of *samekh*.

96. Somewhere between the Sinai and Ethiopia.

[21] It is hidden from the eyes of the living,
Concealed from the birds of the sky.

[22] Abaddon[97] and Death[98] say,
"Our ears have heard something about it."

[23–26] Elohim knows the way there,
He's aware of its location.
For he can look to the ends of the earth,
See all that is under the sky.
When he weighed the weight of the wind,
And measured the measure of water;[99]
And set the amount of the rainfall,
And the path of the thundercloud;

[27] That's when he looked and appraised it,
Measured and examined it.[100]

[28] Then he said to Adam:[101]
"Revering the Lord is wisdom,
And turning from evil, understanding."[102]

---

97. See at 26:6.

98. The personified realm of the dead; see for example 38:17 and Psalm 6:6.

99. Compare Isaiah 40:12–13; Jeremiah 31:36.

100. The deity inspected wisdom like a jeweler a jewel (Habel). Wisdom was created at the beginning of creation; compare Proverbs 8:22–31, some of whose language is used in this passage.

101. The first human or humans; or "to humanity"; the latter interpretation is favored by the Qumran Targum.

102. These are two of Job's qualities; see 1:2. Ironically, Job, not his companions, is here implied to be "wise."

THE DEITY'S FIRST DISCOURSE
(38:1–39:30)

Zophar wished the deity would reveal to Job the source of his suffering (11:5–6), assuming there must be a just cause. Job has made repeated appeals for such a disclosure, insisting that his apparent punishments manifest divine injustice. Job's strategy for compelling the deity to appear and justify what he believes to be the divine charges against him (see especially 13:13–23) was to initiate a lawsuit against the deity and swear that he did not commit any crime that would warrant his extreme afflictions (see Job's Closing Discourse). According to ancient jurisprudence, an oath by one party compels the other party to testify and present the evidence supporting that party's position. Job's strategy succeeds, and the deity appears.

The deity assumes a hostile persona—that of the storm god. Storm gods of the ancient Near East and the storm god persona of the biblical God (see for example Nahum 1:3–6) entail the role of warrior: thunder is a battle cry, lightning bolts are arrows, and so forth (see for example Psalm 18:8–16). Instead of explaining to Job the circumstances of his suffering, as represented in the prologue, the deity addresses Job aggressively, asserting his superiority by demonstrating Job's ignorance. His point is that Job had been making statements about him and his conduct without having direct knowledge of them. Such esoteric knowledge was revealed at the time of creation (compare Prov-

165

erbs 8:22–31), and, as Eliphaz has already intimated (15:7), Job was not then
present. Accordingly, the deity is able to dismiss Job's testimony about him pro
forma—Job lacks the firsthand knowledge of a witness that is required in
order to make the claims in his lawsuit. God extricates himself from the law-
suit without having to explain Job's suffering to him or to his companions.

Most interpreters regard the panorama of creation that the deity displays
as an appropriate response to Job. On the one hand, divine providence is im-
plied; on the other, Job, like other humans, has an exaggerated sense of self-
importance. Nevertheless, it should be borne in mind that Job, acknowledged
as a righteous person, is treated here in bullying fashion. God barely touches
on anything connected to justice or to the providential care of humanity. To
the contrary: he makes rain, which is ordinarily regarded as a divine reward
for good behavior, where no humans can enjoy it; he provides food to preda-
tory animals like the lion and the raven. The exquisite imagery of the divine
discourse portrays a fundamentally amoral world.

[**38:1**] Up speaks YHWH to Job from the windstorm, and he says:

[2] Who is this who obscures good counsel,
(Using) words without knowledge?

[3] Bind up your loins like a man![1]
I will ask you—and you help me know!

[4–6] Where were you when I laid earth's foundations?
Tell me—if you truly know wisdom!
Who set its dimensions? Do you know?
Who stretched the measuring line?

---

1. Preparation for combat.

Into what were its foundations sunk?
Who laid its cornerstone? —
[38] Molding the dirt into solid,
As the clods are stuck together?[2]

[7] When the stars of daybreak sang out,
And the sons of Elohim[3] cheered;[4]

[8–11] He[5] hedged with double-doors Yamm,[6]
As he was gushing out of the womb;
When I gave him cloud as a garment,
Raincloud as his swaddling clothes;
And imposed[7] upon him my boundary.
Setting a bolt 'cross double-doors.[8]
And I said, "This far you may come, but no more!
Here's where I fix[9] the surge of your waves!"

[12–15] Have you ever in your days summoned daybreak,
Made known to the dawning its place?
Holding the earth by its corners,

---

2. This verse clearly belongs here. The copyist overlooked it and wrote it when he noticed, after verse 37 (compare Kahana).

3. The angels; see 1:6.

4. The verse echoes a couplet in a version of Deuteronomy 32:43 preserved in a Qumran scroll: "Sing of his people, all you heavens; pay homage to him, all you divine beings!"

5. The third-person unusually replaces the first-person discourse in this verse, but see 39:17. Some read wa-mi sak "Who hedged . . . ?"

6. The Canaanite sea god; see 3:8; 7:12; 26:13.

7. Reading wa'eshmor "I set as a guard," in keeping with the image and language in 7:12.

8. See 3:10. Note the irony: Job wished he could have been locked in the womb.

9. Reading u-po 'ashit for po' yashit "here (speled unusually with aleph) he fixes."

So the wicked would from it be shaken?[10]
The earth[11] is upturned like the clay in a seal,[12]
And the wicked[13] stand there like a garment;[14]
That the wicked be shed of their "light,"[15]
And the upraised arm be broken.

[16–18] Have you ever reached the sources of Sea,[16]
And walked on the bottom of Ocean?[17]
Were you ever shown the gates of Death,[18]
Or seen the gates of Deathly Shade?
Have you scanned the expanses of earth?
Tell—if you know all of this!

[19–21] On what path dwells the light?
And the darkness—where is its place?
Can you take it to its domain?
Do you know the route to its home?
You must know, for you were born then;
Your number of days is so many![19]

---

10. The earth under cover of darkness is here figured as a blanket, and the wicked are here figured as bugs that infest one's bedding at night (Newsom).

11. Literally, "it."

12. Literally, "a clay seal." When a seal is removed from clay, an image appears.

13. Literally, "they."

14. These lines are difficult, and this particular one is usually emended. For "garment" as an outer skin, see Job 41:5. In the daylight the wicked are visible, like one's outer garment.

15. Night is the wickeds' day, the time they operate; see immediately below and 24:13–17.

16. Yamm (see verse 8).

17. *Tehom,* the Deep (see 28:14).

18. The realm of the dead; see 28:22; compare "the gates of Sheol" in Isaiah 38:10.

19. Returning to the point of verse 4, the deity speaks sarcastically.

[22–23] Have you reached the storerooms of snow?
Have you seen the storerooms of hail?—
I've been saving for a time of distress,
For a day of combat and battle.

[24] By what path is lightning dispensed,
Spreading east winds o'er the land?[20]

[25–27] Who cleaves a downpour's channel,
And a path for the thunderstorm;
To rain down on land without people,
On wilderness with no human in it;[21]
Drenching utter wasteland,
And sprouting grassy growth?

[28–30] Has the rain a progenitor?
Who begot the pools[22] of dew?
From whose womb did ice emerge?
And frost from the sky—who gave it birth?
So water congeals[23] like stone;
The surface of Ocean[24] hardens.

[31–32] Can you tie the bands[25] of the Pleiades,

---

20. For the conjunction of lightning and wind, see Elihu's descriptions in chapter 37.
21. In contradiction to Eliphaz in 5:10 and Elihu in 36:27–28. For the negative connotation of such a wasteland, see Jeremiah 2:6.
22 Compare Arabic ma'jal (Kaddari).
23. From the root ḥb' "to congeal," cognate to ḥem'a "curds," not the common root ḥb' "to hide" (Dhorme).
24. Tehom, the Deep.
25. Compare 1 Samuel 15:32; derived via metathesis from 'anad "to chain."

Or loosen the cords of Orion?[26]
Can you bring the Mazarot[27] out in its season,
Or lead the Hyades with its little ones?

[33–35] Do you know the sky's regularities?
Can you impose their regimen on earth?[28]
Can you raise your voice toward a cloud,
And be covered by a downpour?
Can you send forth lightning bolts,
As they say to you, "Yes, my lord!"?[29]

[36] Who endowed the ibis bird[30] with wisdom,
And gave understanding to the cock?[31]

[37] Who can fill[32] the heavens with wisdom,
And tip the waterskins of the sky?

[39–41] Do you hunt down prey for the lion,

---

26. For these two constellations, see 9:9. The stars of constellations are assumed to be held together by some kind of bond.

27. Probably a variant of *mazal* "constellation." Perhaps Canis Major and Minor (Halpern).

28. Read *mishtaran* "their (for its) regimen," referring to "regularities" (so Kahana).

29. Literally, "here we are"; for this usage, see for example Genesis 22:1, 7, 11; compare Akkadian *anna/u* and postbiblical *hen* "yes."

30. There are several interpretations of these recipients of wisdom. Considering the contrast to the stupid bird in 39:17, I favor the sense of birds. The ibis is associated with the Egyptian god Thot (even if the first consonant in Hebrew is not the usual equivalent of the Egyptian; so Dhorme).

31. So in rabbinic literature. These birds exhibit intelligence; the ibis finds food underground, and the cock discerns the dawn.

32. The verb *sipper* ordinarily means "to relate, inform," but it may here be associated with the term *sipra* "bag, container" (see at 26:13; compare Kahana), and thus "to fill (a bag)."

And quell the hunger of beasts,
As they crouch in their lairs,
Or wait in the thicket to ambush?[33]
Who provides rations to ravens,
When their children cry out to El,
As they wander without food?

The deity questions Job concerning animals that are powerful and wild, while continuing to remind him of his inferiority.

[**39:1–3**] Do you know the season that wild goats give birth?
Or observe the calving of hinds?
Count the months that they gestate?[34]
Know the season they give birth—
As they crouch and deliver their young
Sending forth their offspring?[35]

[4] Their children gain strength and grow up in the wild;
Once they've gone out, they never return.

[5–8] Who sends forth free the wild ass?
The onager—who cuts[36] its cords?
Whose home I made the steppe,
Its habitat the barren land.

---

33. Compare Psalm 10:9.
34. For "filling months" in this sense, compare Genesis 25:24.
35. For *hebel* in this sense, and not "birth pangs," see the cognate verb in the sense of giving birth (for example Psalm 7:15).
36. Literally, "opens, loosens."

He scorns the city's clamor;
Hears not the shouts of a driver.[37]
He surveys[38] the hills for his pasture;
Searches for some vegetation.[39]

[9–12] Will the wild ox[40] want to serve you?
Will he bed down in your crib?
Can you tie the wild ox by rope to a furrow?
Will it harrow the lowland behind you?
Would you rely on him for a full yield,[41]
Leaving your efforts to him?
Would you trust him to bring back[42] your seed,
And collect (the grain) from your threshing-floor?[43]

[13–18] Does[44] the wing of the ostrich[45] flutter?
Does she fly[46] (like the) stork and the falcon?[47]
She abandons her eggs on the ground,[48]

---

37. Compare 3:18: the servant is free from his driver—in death.
38. Reading *yatur* for *yetur* "excess (?)."
39. Literally, "any green."
40. The urus; usually spelled *reʾem*, not *rem*.
41. For this sense of *koaḥ* in Job, see 31:39 (compare Tur-Sinai).
42. Reading *yashib* for *yashub* "he comes back."
43. Would you receive a full return on your seed if the plowing were left to him?
44. Since the following line begins with the interrogative particle *ʾim*, the interrogative particle *ha-* must have dropped out by mistake.
45. Read *yeʿenim* (see Lamentations 4:3) for *renanim* (with change in vocalization) "screechers."
46. The line is variously read. Making no alterations in the consonants, I read *ʾabrah* "it takes wing" for *ʾebrah* "wing." For this verb, see verse 26.
47. Reading *nitsa* (feminine of *nets*; see verse 26) for *we-notsa* "and plumage."
48. I am omitting the particle *ki* "for, since" at the beginning of the line; it would seem to have been copied here by mistake. It would make better sense at the beginning of the following verse. The scribe may have skipped to the next verse, which begins without *ki*, and then, realizing his mistake, continued copying verse 14.

Letting them warm[49] in the dirt;
Forgetful of feet that can trample them,[50]
Of animals that can squash them.
She treats her young harshly as though they're not hers;
She frets not that her effort's for nothing.
For Eloah put wisdom out of her mind
And gave her no share of perception.
And yet she can speed in a run,[51]
Scorning the horse and its rider.[52]

[19–25] Do you give the horse its bravery?[53]
Do you clothe its neck with a mane?[54]
Do you make it noisy as locusts?
The blare[55] of his snorting is fright!
He paws[56] (the ground) with power,[57]
Eager (to ply) his strength,
As he enters into the fray.
He scorns the fearsome, does not flinch;
He does not recoil from the sword:
Even as a quiver[58] whirs by him;

---

49. Incubate.

50. Literally, "it"; there are several exchanges of singular and plural in Job.

51. The verb translated "speed" may be related to an Arabic term for "prodding" a horse. For *marom* "up high" (the ostrich cannot fly), read *merots* "run, race" (Ecclesiastes 9:11).

52. An ostrich can outrun a horse at short distances.

53. *Gebura* may pun on "mane," which is *zuparu* in Akkadian.

54. Interpreted on the basis of context; *rama* suggests "thunder," thereby punning on the next verse. Contrary to what is widely claimed, the word is not the Arabic term for "mane."

55. Reading *hed* "reverberation" for *hod* "splendor." Compare Jeremiah 8:14.

56. Literally, "digs"; reading the singular for the text's plural.

57. Compare in Ugaritic and Akkadian *e-nūcu*. See also Jeremiah 47:3.

58. A quiver's-full of arrows.

Or the blade of a dagger or spear.
With thunder and tremor he laps up the land;[59]
He swerves not at the blast of the horn.
To[60] the horn he answers "hurrah!"
He can smell battle from a distance—
The thunder of captains and battle cries.

[26–30] Does the falcon take flight through your wisdom,
As it spreads its wings toward the south?[61]
Does the eagle fly high at your command,[62]
Or when it nests at an elevation—
Dwelling and bedding in rock,
Protected beneath a cliff?[63]
From there it searches its food;
Its eyes can see from a distance.
Its fledglings swill blood;
Where there is carrion, it is there.

---

59. Literally, "gulps." He keeps advancing; compare Shakespeare: "he seemed in running to devour the way" (*Henry IV, Part 2*, 1:1).

60. On the preposition *badei*, see at 11:3.

61. "South" recalls "Teiman," the region of Eliphaz (see at 2:11).

62. Literally, "mouth."

63. Compare Jeremiah 49:16.

JOB'S RESPONSE TO THE DEITY
(40:1–5)

The deity accosts Job again, but Job has not heard in the deity's first discourse an answer to his demand to learn what he is thought to have done wrong. Accordingly, he places his hand over his mouth, indicating that he is ready to listen and to hear more (see at 21:5 and 29:9).

[**40:**1] Up spoke YHWH to Job and he said:

[2] Should one who censures[1] charge Shaddai?
Should Eloah answer an accuser?

[3] Up spoke Job to YHWH and he said:

---

1. The form *yissor* is a noun formed from *yisser* "to discipline" on the pattern of *gibbor* "brave one."

[4–5] Lacking respect, how can I answer you?
My hand I place over my mouth.
I have spoken once and I will not repeat;[2]
Twice—and I will (speak) no more.

---

2. In view of the next line, read ʾeshneh (see 29:22; so several scholars) for ʾeʿeneh "I will (not) answer."

THE DEITY'S SECOND DISCOURSE
(40:6–41:26)

The deity provides a second response, this time focusing on two creatures, the Behemoth and the Leviathan, of which he is particularly proud. The Behemoth and the Leviathan have been mentioned in the dialogues (see 3:8 and 12:8), but here they are described in extraordinary detail. On the basis of Mesopotamian descriptions of deities, the creatures' being partly composed of inanimate materials suggests a semi-mythological nature—they are more than simply a hippopotamus and a crocodile, beasts native to Egypt. One wonders why God would exhibit these terrifying creatures and challenge Job to tame them.

[**40:6**] Up spoke YHWH to Job from the windstorm, and he said:

[7] Bind up your loins like a man!
I will ask you—and you help me know!

[8] Will you go so far as to breach my justice?

Accuse me of wrong so that you're in the right?¹

[9–13] If you've an arm (as strong as) El's,
And if your voice can thunder like his,
Bedeck yourself with pride and stature,
Clothe yourself with glory and grandeur!
Scatter your raging anger!
Look for the proud and bring him low;
Look for the proud and bend him down!
And crush the wicked where they stand!
Cover them all in the dust;
In the dust² wrap their faces!

[14] Then I myself will praise you,
As your right hand brings you triumph.

[15] Behold now Behemoth,
Which like you I created!

Like large cattle he eats grass.³
[16–18] Behold now the strength in his loins!
The power in his belly's muscles!
He drops⁴ his "tail"⁵ like a cedar (trunk);
The sinews of his testes⁶ intertwine.
His limbs are pipes of bronze,

---

1. For the irony of God making this accusation, see Job 9:30–31.
2. Literally, "the place of covering."
3. This line belongs to verse 15 in the received text.
4. Commonly derived from Arabic *khafada* "to lower."
5. A euphemism for his phallus, which is retracted when inactive.
6. Aramaic.

His bones like an iron rod.[7]

[19–20] He is the first of El's ways;[8]
Only his Maker can prod him with a sword
For the mountains bear him produce,[9]
Where the wild animals play.[10]

[21–22] He lies down under the thornbush,
Under cover of reeds and swamp.
Thornbushes shade him with a thicket;[11]
River willows surround him.

[23] If the river crashes (against him), he will not be alarmed.
He would feel secure were the Jordan to rush in his mouth!

[24] Can one take him as he eyes one?
Can his nose be pierced by barbs?[12]

[25–26] Can you pull the Leviathan with a fish-hook?
Can you bind[13] his tongue with a rope?
Can you place a bulrush 'round its snout.[14]
And pierce its jaw with a hook?

---

7. Aramaic.

8. An ironic allusion to Proverbs 8:22, where the "first of" the deity's "ways" is wisdom!

9. For the motif of bringing tribute to a king in this fashion, see Psalm 72:3.

10. The term for "produce" (ordinarily yebul)—bul—denotes wild animals in Akkadian, suggesting a second meaning for the verse: "Mountain creatures raise (their voices in song) to him; all the wild animals jubilate there" (H. R. Cohen).

11. Literally, "the thornbushes form a thicket above him as shade."

12. Reading bi-qimmosim (see Isaiah 34:13) for bi-moqeshim "with traps," which is inapt.

13. A word known in Samaritan Aramaic read perhaps tishqa' for tashqia' "press down."

14. Tie it closed; compare the Qumran Aramaic translation.

[27–28] Will he make many pleadings to you?
To you will he speak gently?
Will he make a pact with you?[15]
Will he be your slave forever?

[29] Can you toy with him like a bird?[16]
Tie him up (to amuse) your maidens?

[30] Will traders[17] barter over him?
Will they divide him among merchants?[18]

[31–32] Can you cover his hide with prongs,
And his head with a fish harpoon?[19]
Just lay your hand upon him!—
That's the last you will think of battle!

[**41**:1–3] No one's fierce enough to engage[20] him.
Who could take a stand before him?[21]
One's hope (of doing so) is dashed—
At the mere sight of him one's knocked down![22]

---

15. Note the irony in contrasting Eliphaz's promise in 5:23.
16. Compare Psalm 104:26.
17. A unique term, a person who "associates"; cognate *ebarūtu(m)* in Old Assyrian denotes an association of merchants.
18. A regular meaning of the term "Canaanite."
19. The word understood from context to be some sort of harpoon echoes the word for "thornbush" in verses 21–22 above.
20. The verb *'ur* is sometimes used of wielding weapons (see for example 2 Samuel 23:18).
21. Reading *le-panaw* for *le-panay* "before me" (God). Verse 1 belongs syntactically and semantically following verse 2 (so for example Dhorme). The copyist apparently skipped verse 1 by mistake and then copied it following verse 2.
22. For the verb, see Psalm 37:24.

Who has ever confronted him and survived?[23]
Of all that's under heaven—he is mine.

[4] I cannot keep silent about him,
The fact of his incomparable valor.[24]

[5] Who can discover what's under his garb?[25]
Who can penetrate his double armor?[25]

[6] Who can pry open the doors of his face?[27]
All about his teeth is terror!

[7–9] His back[28] is tiers of shields,
Locked like a tight seal.
One reaches up to the other—
No wind could come between them.
Each is stuck onto its brother;
They consolidate and cannot be parted.

[10–13] His sneeze[29] makes a shining light;
His eyes (flash) like glimmers of dawn.

---

23. Literally, "has remained whole." Reading with others on the basis of the Greek: *hiqdimennu . . . wa-yishlam* for *hiqdimani . . . wa'ashallem* "(Who) has confronted/greeted me and I have compensated." Compare 9:4 (in regard to the deity).
24. Reading *geburato* for *geburot* "mighty acts" and *'ein 'erek* "nothing to compare" for *hin 'erko* "the favor (?) of his worth (or arrangement or military array)."
25. Literally, "on the inside (*penim*) of his garment," under his scaly skin.
26. Reading *siryono* (for example Jeremiah 51:3) for *risno* "his bridle" with the ancient translations.
27. His jaws.
28. Reading *gewoh* for *ga'awah* "pride" with the ancient Greek. For the same confusion in the opposite direction, see 22:29.
29. The verb indicates that the singular, not plural, is intended—*atishato*.

Torches proceed from his mouth;
Sparks of fire are emitted.
From his nostrils issues smoke,
As from a cauldron[30] fanned and boiling.[31]
His breathing ignites coals,
As a flame issues from his mouth.

[14–16] In his neck inheres strength;
Power[32] runs[33] ahead of him.[34]
The folds of his flesh stick together;
Forming a solid, it does not slip.
His heart is as solid as rock,
As solid as a bottom millstone.

[17] Even gods live in fear of his majesty;[35]
They're in terror[36] of the ruin he wreaks.[37]

[18–21] One who engages him—(his) sword will fail,[38]
(Likewise) spear, dagger, and dart.[39]
Iron he reckons as hay,

---

30. The Aramaic equivalent of Hebrew *sir* (see Jeremiah 1:13).

31. Reading *ogem* "burning" (so in Arabic) without the final *nun*, which is apparently copied from the beginning of the next word. Compare the description of the deity in Psalm 18:9.

32. Read not *da'abah* "anxiety" but *dob'ah* "power" (Deuteronomy 33:25; and Ugaritic).

33. Reading *taruts* for *taduts* "skips" (a unique Hebrew word drawn from later Aramaic) with the Aramaic version from Qumran.

34. Compare the image in 1 Kings 18:46.

35. Spelled here without *aleph;* compare 13:11.

36. Reading *yeḥattu* for *yithatte'u* "they are cleansed, purified"—compare the usage with *shibbaron* "shattering (disaster)" in Jeremiah 17:18.

37. Reading *shebaraw* "*his* ruinous acts" for *shebarim* "ruinous acts."

38. Literally, "it cannot stand."

39. The latter two terms have cognates in Arabic.

And bronze as rotted wood.
No son of a bow[40] will put him to flight;
Sling stones seem to him straw.[41]
Like straw is reckoned[42] a spear;[43]
He scorns the sound of the javelin.

[22] Beneath him are sharp-edged shards;
He beds down on spikes over clay.

[23–24] He roils the deep like a cauldron;
He treats the sea like a mixing pot.[44]
His wake shines brightly behind him;
The ocean looks[45] to be white-haired!

[25–26] He has no match on earth,
Who is made[46] as fearless as he.
All that is haughty he's got in his view;
Over beasts of all kinds he is king.

---

40. An arrow; compare "sons of the quiver" in Lamentations 3:13.
41. The word "straw" (*qash*) puns on "bow" (*qeshet*).
42. Reading the singular.
43. The unique Hebrew word *totah* has been interpreted variously according to several etymologies, none of which is borne out. In view of the parallel *kidon* "spear, javelin," we should probably read *romah*, a well-attested synonym for "spear, javelin" (compare for example Ball).
44. Ordinarily "an ointment-pot" (BDB). Leviathan's thrashing stirs the water like the mixture in a mortar (compare for example Rashban) Compare the image in Ezekiel 32:2.
45. Reading *yehasheb* "it is reckoned" for *yahshob* "he reckons" (Dillmann).
46. The passive participle *'asu* for *'asuy*, if not an error, is archaic (Gordis, *Book of Job*).

JOB'S RESPONSE TO THE DEITY
(42:1–6)

Job understands the deity to be exactly as he had feared: a purveyor of power who cares little for people. Parodying the divine discourse through mimicry, Job expresses disdain toward the deity and pity toward humankind (and not acquiescence, as has been generally thought; see the introduction).

[**42:1**] Up spoke Job to YHWH and he said:

[2] I have known you are able to do all;
That you cannot be blocked from any scheme.[1]

[3] "Who is this hiding[2] counsel without knowledge?"[3]

---

1. Job speaks of the deity in the disdainful terms that God had spoken of the builders of the Tower of Babel (Genesis 11:6).
2. If a similar Arabic verb is evoked, there is a double entendre: "make known."
3. Job mimics the deity in 38:2.

Truly I've spoken without comprehending—
Wonders beyond me that I do not know.[4]

[4] "Hear now and I will speak!
I will ask you, and you help me know!"[5]

[5] As a hearing by the ear I have heard you,
And now my eye has seen you.[6]

[6] That is why I am fed up;[7]
I take pity[8] on "dust and ashes!"[9]

---

4. A mock concession.

5. Job mimics the deity in 38:3; 40:7.

6. A mock concession; Job has already said this (13:1).

7. For *ma'as* used intransitively in the sense of being "fed up," see 7:16.

8. See for example 2 Samuel 13:39; Psalm 90:13.

9. "Dust and ashes" is a figure for wretched humanity; see its two other occurrences in Genesis 18:27 and Job 30:19

EPILOGUE
(42:7-17)

The narrative resumes in prose. In a radical surprise, the deity chastens Job's companions for failing to speak "honestly," as had Job (see the introduction). Only Job's intercession on their behalf can secure their pardon. God restores Job's fortunes twofold and replaces the ten children he had lost. In another extraordinary gesture, special attention is paid to Job's three daughters, who are also given a share of his estate (compare Numbers 27:1–11). No mention is made of Job's wife, the Satan, or the curing of Job's disease. One may surmise that his health is restored because he is blessed in every other way and lives a long life. The significance of Job's restoration is ambiguous: perhaps he passed the test and was not thought to have cursed God; or perhaps the test is simply over, and he is returned to his pretrial status.

[**42:7-8**] It happened, after YHWH spoke these words to Job, that YHWH said to Eliphaz the Teimanite:

"I am angry at you and your two companions,[1]
for you did not speak about[2] me in honesty[3] as did my servant Job.
Now then, take yourselves seven bulls and seven rams and go to
my servant Job,
and offer up a burnt-offering on your own behalf;
and my servant Job will pray for you;
for I will lift up his face without doing anything unseemly to you—
for you did not speak about me in honesty as did my servant Job."

[9–10] So they went, Eliphaz the Teimanite and Bildad the Shuhite
and[4] Zophar the Na'amathite, and they did as YHWH had
spoken to them;
And YHWH lifted up Job's face.
For YHWH had restored Job's restoration when he had prayed for
his companions.
YHWH added double to what Job had had.[5]

[11] Then they came to him, all his brothers and all his sisters and
all his friends from beforehand,
and they ate a meal with him in his house,
and they shook-their-heads-in-pity and they consoled him for all
the evil that YHWH had brought upon him;

---

1. The latecomer Elihu is not included; see the introduction to his discourses.
2. For the preposition 'el in the sense of 'a', see for example Jeremiah 40:16.
3. Compare ken "honest, truthful" in Genesis 41:32. The friends relied on traditional wisdom instead of the knowledge that is learned from experience (including revelation).
4. The conjunction is missing in the Hebrew, but it should be restored.
5. A twofold restoration is required of thieves (Exodus 22:3). It may be inferred that the removal of Job's property was a wrongful act. Or perhaps it is for consolation.

and they each gave him one chip-of-silver[6] and one gold ring.[7]

[12–15] So YHWH blessed Job's latter-life more than his
former-life.
He came to have fourteen thousand small cattle and six thousand
camels and a thousand yoke of large cattle and a thousand
she-asses.
And he came to have seven sons and three daughters.
He called the name of the first Yemima/Turtle-Dove and the name
of the second Ketsiah/Cassia and the name of the third Keren
Ha-Pukh/Horn of Kohl.[8]
One could not find women as fair as Job's daughters in all the land;
and he, their father, gave them an inheritance in the midst of their
brothers.[9]

[16–17] After this Job lived one hundred and forty years.
He saw his sons and his sons' sons—four generations.[10]
Job died old and sated with days.[11]

------

6. An archaic unit of payment (see Genesis 33:19). It may be derived from a verb
meaning "to chip off," like *qashata* in Arabic (compare *qushata* "chip").
7. A ring for the ear or nose.
8. Mascara; cosmetics were kept in a horn.
9. Like that of their brothers (Machinist); see Numbers 27:7.
10. Like a patriarch; see Genesis 50:23.
11. Like a patriarch; see Genesis 35:29.

References and Select Bibliography

The Author's Publications on or Touching on Job

"Aramaisms in the Bible. I. Hebrew Bible/Old Testament." In *Encyclopedia of the Bible and Its Reception*, ed. Hans-Josef Klauck et al., vol. 2, cols. 630–34. Berlin: W. de Gruyter, 2009.

"Bildad Lectures Job: A Close Reading of Job 8." In *Close Readings of Biblical Hebrew Poems*, ed. J. Blake Couey and Elaine James, 63–79. New York: Cambridge University Press, 2018.

"The Book of Job" (introduction and annotations). In *The Jewish Study Bible*, 2nd ed., ed. Adele Berlin and Marc Z. Brettler, 1489–1556. New York: Oxford University Press, 2014.

"The Book of Job and Mesopotamian Literature: How Many Degrees of Separation?" In *Citation, Allusion, and Translation in the Hebrew Bible*, ed. Ziony Zevit, 143–58. London: Equinox Press, 2017.

"Challenges in Translating the Book of Job." In *Found In Translation: Essays on Jewish Biblical Translation in Honor of Leonard J. Greenspoon*, ed. James W. Barker, Anthony Le Donne, and Joel N. Lohr, 179–99. West Lafayette: Purdue University Press, 2018.

" 'Difficulty' in the Poetry of Job." In *A Critical Engagement: Essays on the Hebrew Bible in Honour of J. Cheryl Exum*, ed. David J. A. Clines and Ellen van Wolde, 186–95. Sheffield: Sheffield Phoenix Press, 2011.

"The Extent of Job's First Speech." In *Studies in Bible and Biblical Exegesis, 7, Presented to Menachem Cohen*, ed. Shmuel Vargon et al., 245–62. Ramat-Gan, Israel: Bar-Ilan University Press, 2005 [Hebrew with English abstract].

"Features of Language in the Poetry of Job." In *Das Buch Hiob und seine*

Interpretationen, ed. Thomas Krüger et al., 81–96. Zurich: Theologischer Verlag Zürich, 2007.

"A Forensic Understanding of the Speech from the Whirlwind." In *Texts, Temples, and Traditions: A Tribute to Menahem Haran,* ed. Michael V. Fox et al., 241–58. Winona Lake, IN: Eisenbrauns, 1996.

"God's Test of Job." In *Shai le-Sara Japhet: Studies in the Bible, Its Exegesis and Its Language,* ed. Moshe Bar-Asher et al., 263–72. Jerusalem: Mossad Bialik, 2007 [Hebrew].

"The Heart as an Organ of Speech in Biblical Hebrew." In *Festschrift for Richard C. Steiner,* ed. Mordechai Z. Cohen, Aaron Koller, and Adina Moshavi. New York: Yeshiva University / Jerusalem: Mossad Bialik, forthcoming.

"How Does Parallelism Mean?" In *A Sense of Text. Jewish Quarterly Review Supplement,* (1983): 41–70.

"In Job's Face / Facing Job." In *The Labour of Reading: Desire, Alienation, and Biblical Interpretation* (Festschrift for Robert C. Culley), ed. Fiona C. Black et al., 301–17. Atlanta: Scholars Press, 1999.

"The Invention of Language in the Poetry of Job." In *Interested Readers: Essays on the Hebrew Bible in Honor of David J. A. Clines,* ed. James K. Aitken, Jeremy M. S. Clines, and Christl M. Maier, 331–46. Atlanta: Society of Biblical Literature, 2013.

"Jeremiah as an Inspiration to the Poet of Job." In *Inspired Speech: Prophecy in the Ancient Near East—Essays in Honor of Herbert B. Huffmon,* ed. John Kaltner and Louis Stulman, 98–110. London and New York: T. and T. Clark International / Continuum, 2004.

"Job." In *The Routledge Encyclopedia of Ancient Mediterranean Religions,* ed. Eric Orlin, 482. London: Routledge, 2016.

"The Job of Translating Job." *Association for Jewish Studies Newsletter* 30 (October 1981): 6–7.

"Job's Wife—Was She Right after All?" *Beit Mikra* 178 (2004): 19–31 [Hebrew with English abstract].

"The Language of the Book of Job: Characterizing Its Features." In *Proceedings of the Conference on Biblical Hebrew.* Jerusalem: Israel Academy for the Hebrew Language, forthcoming [Hebrew].

"The Language of Job and Its Poetic Function." *Journal of Biblical Literature* 122 (2003): 651–66.

"The Loneliness of Job." In *The Book of Job in Scripture, Thought, and Art,* ed. Lea Mazor, 43–53. Jerusalem: Mount Scopus Publications, 1995 [Hebrew].

"Metaphors of Illness and Wellness in the Book of Job." In *"When the Morning Stars Sang": Essays in Honor of Choon Leong Seow on the Occasion of His*

Sixty-Fifth Birthday, ed. Scott C. Jones and Christine Roy Yoder, 39–50. Berlin: W. de Gruyter, 2018.

"'On My Skin and in My Flesh': Personal Experience as a Source of Knowledge in the Book of Job." In *Bringing the Hidden to Light: Studies in Honor of Stephen A. Geller*, ed. Kathryn F. Kravitz and Diane M. Sharon, 63–77. New York: The Jewish Theological Seminary / Winona Lake, IN: Eisenbrauns, 2007.

"On the Prefixed Preterite in Biblical Hebrew." *Hebrew Studies* 29 (1988): 7–17.

"On the Use of Akkadian in Biblical Hebrew Philology." In *Looking at the Ancient Near East and the Bible through the Same Eyes: A Tribute to Aaron Skaist*, ed. Kathleen Abraham and Joseph Fleishman, 335–53. Bethesda, MD: CDL Press, 2012.

"Parody as a Challenge to Tradition: The Use of Deuteronomy 32 in the Book of Job." In *Reading Job Intertextually*, ed. Katharine J. Dell and Will Kynes, 66–78 (plus bibliography). London: Bloomsbury / T. and T. Clark, 2012.

"The Poem on Wisdom in Job 28 in Its Conceptual and Literary Contexts." In *Job 28: Cognition in Context*, ed. Ellen van Wolde, 253–80. Leiden: Brill, 2003.

"The Poetic Use of Akkadian in the Book of Job." In *The Avi Hurvitz Festschrift* (*Mehqarim be-Lashon* 11–12), ed. Steven E. Fassberg and Aharon Mamar., 51–68. Jerusalem: Magnes Press, 2008 [Hebrew with English abstract].

"The Problem of Evil in the Book of Job." In *Mishneh Todah: Studies in Deuteronomy and Its Cultural Environment in Honor of Jeffrey H. Tigay*, ed. Nili S. Fox et al., 333–62. Winona Lake, IN: Eisenbrauns, 2009.

"Professor Robert Gordis and the Literary Approach to Bible." *Proceedings of the Rabbinical Assembly* 48 (1986): 190–200.

"Proverbs and Popular Sayings, Real or Invented, in the Book of Job." In *Teaching Morality in Antiquity: Wisdom Texts, Oral Traditions, and Images*, ed. Takayoshi Oshima with Susanne Kohlhaas, 137–49. Tübingen: Mohr Siebeck, 2018.

"Remarks on Some Metaphors in the Book of Job." In *Studies in Bible and Exegesis, 9, Presented to Moshe Garsiel*, ed. Shmu'el Vargon et al., 231–41. Ramat-Gan, Israel: Bar-Ilan University Press, 2009 [Hebrew with English abstract].

Reply concerning "When Job Sued God." *Biblical Archaeology Review* 38, no. 5 (September/October 2012): 9.

Review of *Rumors of Wisdom: Job 28 as Poetry, Review of Biblical Literature* (online) 7/2012 (4 pp.). https://www.bookreviews.org/bookdetail.asp?TitleId=8209

Review of *Talking about God: Job 42:7–9 and the Nature of God in the Book of*

References and Select Bibliography

Job, Review of Biblical Literature (online) 7/2004 (4 pp.). https://www.book reviews.org/bookdetail.asp?TitleId=3195

Review of *The Vision in Job 4 and Its Function in the Book. AJS [Association for Jewish Studies] Review* 42 (2018): 197–200.

Review of *"You Have Not Spoken What Is Right about Me": Intertextuality and the Book of Job. Review of Biblical Literature* (online) 11/2003 (4 pp.). https://www.bookreviews.org/bookdetail.asp?TitleId=3093

"Some Chapters in the Biography of Job." In *Studies in Bible and Exegesis* 10, *Presented to Shmuel Vargon,* ed. Moshe Garsiel et al., 385–401. Ramat-Gan, Israel: Bar-Ilan University Press, 2011 [Hebrew with English abstract].

"Some Metaphors in the Poetry of Job." In *Built by Wisdom, Established by Understanding: Essays on Biblical and Near Eastern Literature in Honor of Adele Berlin,* ed. Maxine L. Grossman, 179–95. Bethesda, MD: CDL Press, 2013 [revised version of a Hebrew article published in 2009].

"Theories of Modern Bible Translation." *Prooftexts* 3 (1983): 9–39.

"Three Philological Notes on the Book of Job." In *Zer Rimmonim: Studies in Biblical Literature and Exegesis Presented to Professor Rimon Kasher,* ed. Michael Avioz, Elie Assis, and Yael Shemesh, 297–308. Atlanta: Society of Biblical Literature, 2013 [Hebrew with English abstract].

"Truth or Theodicy? Speaking Truth to Power in the Book of Job." *Princeton Seminary Bulletin* 27 (2006): 238–58.

"When Job Sued God." *Biblical Archaeology Review* 38, no. 3 (May/June 2012): 55–57, 60.

"Wisdom in the Book of Job—Undermined." In *Wisdom, Her Pillars Are Seven: Studies in Biblical, Post-Biblical and Ancient Near Eastern Wisdom Literature (Beer-sheva 20),* ed. Shamir Yona and Victor Avigdor Hurowitz, 41–50. Beer-sheva: Ben-Gurion University of the Negev Press, 2011 [Hebrew with English abstract].

"Wisdom Literature." In *The Routledge Encyclopedia of Ancient Mediterranean Religions,* ed. Eric Orlin, 1002–3. London: Routledge, 2016.

Works Cited and Selected Additional Publications

Abegg, Martin, Jr., Peter Flint, and Eugene Ulrich. *The Dead Sea Scrolls Bible.* San Francisco: HarperCollins, 1999.

Anat, Moshe. *The People's Bible: Psalms, Proverbs, Job.* Tel Aviv: Am Oved, 1974 [Hebrew].

Ayali-Darshan, Noga. "The Question of the Order of Job 26:7–13 and the Cosmogonic Tradition of Zaphon." *Zeitschrift für die alttestamentliche Wissenschaft* 126 (2014): 402–17.

Bailey, Clinton. *Bedouin Culture in the Bible.* New Haven and London: Yale
University Press, 2018.

Ball, C. J. *The Book of Job: A Revised Text and Version.* Oxford: Clarendon,
1922.

Barr, James. "Hebrew Orthography and the Book of Job." *Journal of Semitic
Studies* 30 (1985): 1–33.

BDB = Francis Brown, S. R. Driver, and Charles A. Briggs. *A Hebrew and
English Lexicon of the Old Testament.* Oxford: Clarendon, 1907.

Blommerde, Anton. *Northwest Semitic Grammar and Job.* Rome: Pontifical
Biblical Institute, 1969.

Brenton, Lancelot C. L. *The Septuagint with Apocrypha: Greek and English.*
Grand Rapids, MI: Zondervan, 1983.

Brown, Ken. *The Vision in Job 4 and Its Role in the Book.* Tübingen: Mohr
Siebeck, 2015.

Brown, William P. "*Creatio Corporis* and the Rhetoric of Defense in Job 10 and
Psalm 139." In *God Who Cares: Essays in Honor of W. Sibley Towner,* ed.
William P. Brown and S. Dean McBride Jr., 107–24. Grand Rapids, MI:
W. B. Eerdmans, 2000.

Buber, Martin. *Die Schriftwerke.* vol. 4. Heidelberg: Lambert Schneider, 1986.

Budde, Karl. *Das Buch Hiob.* Göttingen: Vandenhoeck and Ruprecht, 1913

Cheney, Michael. *Dust, Wind and Agony: Character, Speech and Genre in Job.*
Stockholm: Almqvist and Wicksell International, 1994.

Clines, David J. A. *Job 1–20.* Dallas: Word, 1989.

———. *Job 21–37.* Nashville: Thomas Nelson, 2006.

———. *Job 38–42.* Nashville: Thomas Nelson, 2009.

———. " 'The Fear of the Lord is Wisdom' (Job 28:28): A Semantic and Contextual Study." In *Job 28: Cognition in Context,* ed. Ellen van Wolde, 57–92.
Leiden: Brill, 2003.

Cohen, Harold R. (Chaim). *Hapax Legomena in the Light of Akkadian and
Ugaritic.* Missoula, MT: Scholars Press, 1978.

Cohen, Menachem, ed. *Miqra'ot Gedolot "Ha-Keter."* Ramat-Gan: Bar-Ilan
University; on-line edition [Hebrew].

Cohen, Yoram. *Wisdom from the Late Bronze Age.* Atlanta: Society of Biblical
Literature, 2013.

Cooley, Jeffrey L. *Poetic Astronomy in the Ancient Near East: The Reflexes of
Celestial Science in Ancient Mesopotamian, Ugaritic, and Israelite Narrative.*
Winona Lake, IN: Eisenbrauns, 2013.

Course, John E. *Speech and Response: A Rhetorical Analysis of the Introductions
to the Speeches of the Book of Job (Chaps. 4–14).* Washington, DC: Catholic
Biblical Association of America, 1994.

Curtis, John B. "On Job's Response to Yahweh." *Journal of Biblical Literature* 98 (1979): 497–511.

De Moor, Johannes C. "Ugarit and the Origin of Job." In *Ugarit and the Bible*, ed. George J. Brooke, Adrian H. Curtis, and John Healey, 225–57. Münster: Ugarit-Verlag, 1994.

Dell, Katharine J. *The Book of Job as Sceptical Literature*. Berlin: W. de Gruyter, 1991.

Dell, Katharine, and Will Kynes, eds. *Reading Job Intertextually*. New York: Bloomsbury, 2013.

Dentith, Simon. *Parody*. London: Routledge, 2000.

Dhorme, Edouard. *A Commentary on the Book of Job*. Translated by Harold Knight. London. Thomas Nelson and Sons, 1967.

Dick, Michael B. "Job 31: The Oath of Innocence and the Sage." *Zeitschrift für die alttestamentliche Wissenschaft* 95 (1983): 31–53.

Dillmann, August. *Hiob*. 4th ed. Leipzig: S. Hirzel, 1891.

Driver, Samuel R., and George B. Gray. *A Critical and Exegetical Commentary on the Book of Job*. 2 vols. New York: Scribner's, 1921.

Duhm, Bernard. *Das Buch Hiob*. Freiburg: Mohr, 1897.

Ehrlich, Arnold B. *Randglossen zur hebräischen Bibel*, vol. 6. Reprint: Hildesheim: Ohms, 1968.

Finkelstein, J. J. "Hebrew *ḥbr* and Semitic **ḫbr*." *Journal of Biblical Literature* 75 (1956): 328–31.

Fishbane, Michael. "The Book of Job and Inner-Biblical Discourse." In *The Voice from the Whirlwind: Interpreting the Book of Job*, ed. Leo G. Perdue and W. Clark Gilprin, 86–98. Nashville: Abingdon, 1992.

Fohrer, Georg. *Das Buch Hiob*. Gütersloh: Gütersloher Verlagshaus Gerd Mohn, 1963.

Folmer, M. L. *The Aramaic Language in the Achaemenid Period: A Study in Linguistic Variation*. Leuven: Peeters, 1995.

Fontaine, Carol R. *Traditional Sayings in the Old Testament: A Contextual Study*. Sheffield: Sheffield Academic Press, 1982.

Fox, Michael V. "The Identification of Quotations in Biblical Literature." *Zeitschrift für die alttestamentliche Wissenschaft* 92 (1980): 416–31.

Freedman, Leslie R. "Biblical Hebrew '*rb*, 'to go surety', and Its Nominal Forms." *Journal of the Ancient Near Eastern Society* 19 (Semitic Studies in Memory of Moshe Held; 1989): 25–29.

Fullerton, Kemper. "Double Entendre in the First Speech of Eliphaz." *Journal of Biblical Literature* 49 (1930): 320–74.

Fyall, Robert S. *Now My Eyes Have Seen You: Images of Creation and Evil in the Book of Job*. Downers Grove, IL: Apollos/InterVarsity Press, 2002.

References and Select Bibliography

Geller, Stephen A. "'Where Is Wisdom?': A Literary Study of Job 23 in Its Settings." In *Judaic Perspectives on Ancient Israel*, ed. Jacob Neusner, Baruch A. Levine, and Ernest Frerichs, 155–88. Philadelphia: Fortress, 1987.

Gersonides = R. Levi ben Gershom. See Coner, ed

Gesenius, Wilhelm. *Gesenius' Hebrew Grammar*. Edited and enlarged by E. Kautzsch. 2nd English ed. by A. E. Cowley. Oxford: Clarendon, 1910.

Ginsberg, H. L. "Studies in the Book of Job." *Lešonénu* 21 (1958): 259–64 [Hebrew].

———. "An Unrecognized Allusion to Kings Pekah and Hoshea of Israel (Isaiah 8:23)." *Eretz-Israel* 5 (Benjamin Mazar Volume 1959): 61*–65*.

———. "Job the Patient and Job the Impatient." *Vetus Testamentum Supplement* 17 (1969): 88–111.

———. "Job, the Book of." *Encyclopedia Judaica*. Jerusalem: Keter, 1972, vol. 10, cols. 111–21.

Good, Edwin M. *In Turns of Tempest: A Reading of Job with a Translation*. Stanford: Stanford University Press, 1990.

Gordis, Robert. "Hebrew Roots of Contrasted Meanings." *Jewish Quarterly Review* 27 (1936): 33–58.

———. *The Book of Job: Commentary, New Translation, and Special Studies*. New York: Jewish Theological Seminary of America, 1978.

Gray, John. *The Book of Job*. Edited by David J. A Clines. Sheffield: Sheffield Phoenix Press, 2010.

Greenspahn, Frederick E. "A Mesopotamian Proverb and Its Biblical Reverberations." *Journal of the American Oriental Society* 114 (1994): 33–38.

Guillaume, A. *Studies in the Book of Job with a New Translation*. Edited by J. Macdonald. Leiden: Brill, 1968.

Habel, Norman C. *The Book of Job: A Commentary*. Philadelphia: Westminster, 1985.

Hackett, Jo Ann. *The Balaam Text from Deir 'Allā*. Chico, CA: Scholars Press, 1980.

Hakham, Amos. *The Book of Job*. Jerusalem Mossad Ha-Rav Kook, 1970 [Hebrew].

HALOT = Ludwig Koehler and Walter Baumgartner. *The Hebrew and Aramaic Lexicon of the Old Testament*. Revised by Walter Baumgartner and Johann J. Stamm. Translated and edited by M. E. J. Richardson. Leiden: Brill, 2001.

Halpern, Baruch. "Assyrian and Pre-Socratic Astronomies and the Location of the Book of Job." In *Kein Land für sich allein* (Festschrift for Manfred Weippert), ed. Ulrich Hübner and Ernst A. Knauf, 255–64 Freiburg: University Press / Göttingen: Vandenhoeck and Ruprecht, 2002.

Hartley, John E. *The Book of Job*. Grand Rapids, MI: W. B Eerdmans, 1988.

Hayyut (Chajes), Zvi Peretz. *Psalms*. The Tanakh with a Scientific Commentary, ed. A. Kahana. Zhitomer: Avraham Kahana, 1902 [Hebrew].

Held, Moshe. "Pits and Pitfalls in Akkadian and Biblical Hebrew." *Journal of the Ancient Near Eastern Society* 5 (The Gaster Festschrift; 1973): 173–90.

———. "Studies in Biblical Lexicography in the Light of Akkadian, Part 2." In *Studies in Bible Dedicated to the Memory of U. Cassuto on the 100th Anniversary of His Birth*, ed. S. E. Loewenstamm, 104–26. Jerusalem: Magnes Press, 1987 [Hebrew].

Hoffman, Yair. *A Blemished Perfection*. Translated by Jonathan Chipman. Sheffield: Sheffield Academic Press, 1996.

Holtz, Shalom E. "Why Are the Sins of Ephraim (Hos 13,12) and Job (Job 14,17) Bundled?" *Biblica* 93 (2012): 107–15.

Hurvitz, Avi. "The Date of the Prose-Tale of Job Linguistically Reconsidered." *Harvard Theological Review* 67 (1974): 17–34.

Ibn Ezra = R. Abraham Ibn Ezra, Commentary on the Book of Job. See Cohen, ed.

Ibn Janah, Abulwalid Merwan (R. Jonah). *The Book of Roots*. Edited by Wilhelm Bacher. Berlin: Itzkowski, 1896 [Hebrew].

Jastrow, Marcus. *A Dictionary of the Targumim.* . . . 2 vols. Reprint: New York: Judaica Press, 1996.

Joosten, Jan. "Linguistic Clues as to the Date of the Book of Job: A Mediating Position." In *Interested Readers: Essays on the Hebrew Bible in Honor of David J. A. Clines*, ed. James K. Aitken, Jeremy M. S. Clines, and Christl M. Maier, 347–57. Atlanta: Society of Biblical Literature; 2013.

Kaddari, Menahem Zevi. *A Dictionary of Biblical Hebrew*. Ramat-Gan: Bar-Ilan University Press, 2006 [Hebrew].

Kahana, Avraham. *The Book of Job*. Torah Nevi'im u-Ketuvim 'im perush madda'i. Tel Aviv: Meqorot, 1928 [Hebrew].

Kara = Moshe Ahrend, ed. *The Commentary of R. Joseph Kara to the Book of Job*. Jerusalem: Mossad Ha-Rav Kook, 1988 [Hebrew].

Kimhi, David. *The Book of Roots*. Edited by J. H. R. Biesenthal and F. Lebrecht. Berlin: G. Bethge, 1847 [Hebrew].

Kimhi, Moses. *Commentary on the Book of Job*. Edited with an introduction by Herbert Basser and Barry D. Walfish. Atlanta: Scholars Press, 1992.

Kister, Menachem. "Some Blessing and Curse Formulae in the Bible, Northwest Semitic Inscriptions, Post-Biblical Literature and Late Antiquity." In *Hamlet on a Hill* (Festschrift for T. Muraoka), ed. M. F. J. Baasten and W. Th. van Peursen, 313–32. Leuven: Peeters, 2003.

Kittel, Rudolf, ed. *Biblia Hebraica*. Stuttgart: Württembergische Bibelanstalt, 1937.

References and Select Bibliography

Kopf, L. "Arabische Etymologien und Parallelen zum Bibelwörterbuch." *Vetus Testamentum* 8 (1958): 161–215.

Lévêque, Jean. "Le sens de la suffrance d'après le livre de Job." *Revue Théologique de Louvain* 6 (1975): 438–59.

Livingstone, Alasdair. *Mystical and Mythological Explanatory Works of Assyrian and Babylonian Scholars.* Oxford: Clarendon. 1986.

Luzzatto, Samuel David. *The Commentaries of Shadal [S. D. Luzzatto] to Jeremiah, Ezekiel, Proverbs, and Job.* Lemberg: A. Isaak Menkes, 1876 [Hebrew].

Machinist, Peter. "Job's Daughters and Their Inheritance in the Testament of Job and Its Biblical Congeners." In *The Echoes of Many Texts: Reflections on Jewish and Christian Traditions in Honor of Lou H. Silberman,* ed. William G. Dever and J. Edward Wright, 67–80. Atlanta: Scholars Press, 1997.

Magdalene, F. Rachel. *On the Scales of Righteousness: Neo-Babylonian Trial Law and the Book of Job.* Providence: Brown Judaic Studies, 2007.

Malbim = R. Meir Leibush ben Yehiel Mikhl Wisser. In *Miqra'ot Gedolot,* vol. 9. New York: M. P. Press, 1980 [Hebrew].

Mandelkern, Solomon. *Concordance to the Tanakh.* 7th ed. Jerusalem-Tel Aviv: Schocken, 1967 [Hebrew].

Mangan, Céline. "The Targum of Job." In *The Aramaic Bible, 15: The Targum of Job, The Targum of Proverbs, The Targum of Qohelet,* ed. Kevin Cathcart, Michael Maher, and Martin McNamara, ix–93. Collegeville, MN: Liturgical Press, 1991.

Masnuth = R. Samuel ben R. Nissim Masnuth. *Ma'yan Ganim, A Commentary on the Book of Job according to the Peshat.* Edited by Solomon Buber. Berlin: Meqitsei Nirdamim, 1889 [Hebrew].

Meyuhhas = *The Commentary of Rabbenu Meyuhhas ben Eliyahu on the Book of Job.* Edited by Hayyim Dov Chavel. Jerusalem: Feldheim, 1970 [Hebrew].

Millard, A. R. "What Has No Taste? (Job 6:6)." *Ugarit-Forschungen* 1 (1969): 210.

Montgomery, James A. *Aramaic Incantation Texts from Nippur.* Philadelphia: University Museum, 1913.

Muraoka, Takamitsu, and Bezalel Porten. *A Grammar of Egyptian Aramaic.* Leiden: Brill, 1998.

Nahmanides (R. Moses ben Nahman). *Peirushei Ramban 'al Nevi'im u-Khetuvim.* Edited by Hayyim Dov Chavel. Jerusalem: Horev, 1986.

Newsom, Carol A. *The Book of Job. New Interpreter's Bible,* 4:317–637. Nashville: Abingdon, 1996.

Oshima, Takayoshi. *Babylonian Poems of Pious Sufferers.* Tübingen: Mohr Siebeck, 2014.

Paul, Shalom M. "Unrecognized Biblical Legal Idioms in the Light of Comparative Akkadian Expressions." *Revue biblique* 36 (1979): 231–39.

Pfeffer, Jeremy I. *Malbim's Job*. Jersey City, NJ: Ktav, 2003.

Pope, Marvin H. *Job*. 3rd ed. Garden City, NY: Doubleday, 1973.

Rabinowitz, A. Z., and A. Avrunin. *Job*. Jaffa: Saadia Shoshani, 1916 [Hebrew].

Rashbam = Sara Japhet. *The Commentary of R. Samuel ben Meir (Rashbam) to the Book of Job*. Jerusalem: Magnes Press, 2000 [Hebrew].

Rashi = Avraham Shoshana, ed. *The Book of Job according to the School of Rashi*. Jerusalem: Machon Ofek, 2000 [Hebrew].

Rowley, H. H. *The Book of Job*. Grand Rapids, MI: W. B. Eerdmans / London: Morgan and Scott, 1976.

Saadia Gaon = Yosef Kapah, ed. *Job with the Translation and Commentary of Rav Saadia Gaon*. Israel: Committee for the Publication of Works of R. Saadia Gaon, 1973 [Hebrew]; Lenn E. Goodman, *The Book of Theodicy . . . by Saadiah Ben Joseph Al-Fayyūmī*. New Haven-London: Yale University Press, 1988.

Sarna, Nahum M. "Notes on the Use of the Definite Article in the Poetry of Job." In *Texts, Temples, and Traditions: A Tribute to Menahem Haran*, ed. Michael V. Fox et al., 279–84. Winona Lake, IN: Eisenbrauns, 1996.

Scheindlin, Raymond P. *The Book of Job: Translation, Introduction, and Notes*. New York: W. W. Norton, 1998.

Segal, Moshe Zvi. "Parallels in the Book of Job." *Tarbiz* 20 (1949): 35–48 [Hebrew].

Seow, Choon Leong. *Job 1–21: Interpretation and Commentary*. Grand Rapids, MI: W. B. Eerdmans, 2013.

Snaith, Norman H. *The Book of Job: Its Origin and Purpose*. London: SCM Press, 1968.

Sokoloff, Michael. *The Targum to Job from Qumran Cave XI*. Ramat-Gan: Bar-Ilan University Press, 1974.

Spiegel, Shalom. "Noah, Daniel, and Job, Touching on Canaanite Relics in the Legends of the Jews." In *Louis Ginzberg Jubilee Volume, 305–55*. New York: American Academy for Jewish Research, 1946.

Spivak, Gayatri Chakravorty. "The Politics of Translation." In *Outside in the Teaching Machine*, 179–200. New York: Routledge, 1993.

Szczygiel, Paul. *Das Buch Hiob*. Bonn: Hanstein, 1931.

Szold, Benjamin. *The Book of Job*. Baltimore: H. F. Siemers, 1886 [Hebrew].

Terrien, Samuel. *Job*. Neuchatel: Editions Delachaux and Niestlé, 1963.

Tov, Emanuel. "Job 34 [in the Septuagint]." In *Outside the Bible: Ancient Jewish Writings Related to Scripture*, ed. Louis H. Feldman, James L. Kugel, and Lawrence H. Schiffman, 11–14. Lincoln: University of Nebraska Press, 2013.

Tur-Sinai, N. H. *The Book of Job: A New Commentary*. Revised edition. Jerusalem Kiryath Sepher, 1967.

Vall, Gregory R. "From Womb to Tomb: Poetic Imagery and the Book of Job." Ph.D. diss., Catholic University of America Washington, DC, 1993.

Waltke, Bruce K., and M. O'Connor. *An Introduction to Biblical Hebrew Syntax.* Winona Lake, IN: Eisenbrauns, 1990.

Weber, Henry J. "Material for the Construction of a Grammar of the Book of Job." *American Journal of Semitic Languages and Literatures* 15 (1898): 1–32.

Wehr, Hans. *A Dictionary of Modern Written Arabic*. Edited by J. Milton Cowan. Ithaca: Cornell University Press, 1966.

Weinfeld, Moshe. "'Partition, Partition; Wall, Wall, Listen': 'Leaking' the Divine Secret to Someone Behind the Curtain." *Archiv für Orientforschung* 44–45 (1997–98): 222–25.

Weiss, Raphael. "On Ligatures in the Hebrew Bible." *Journal of Biblical Literature* 82 (1963): 188–94.

———. *The Aramaic Targum of Job*. Tel Aviv: Tel Aviv University, 1979 [Hebrew with English summary].

Wiseman, Donald J. *The Alalakh Tablets*. London: British School of Archaeology at Ankara, 1953.

Witte. Markus. *Philologische Notizen zu Hiob 21–27*. Berlin: W. de Gruyer, 1995.

Yellin, David. *Hiqrei miqra'* [Biblical Studies] 1 *Job*. Jerusalem: Zion Press, 1927 [Hebrew].

Zalcman, Lawrence. "An Unnoticed Pun at Job 20,7." *Zeitschrift für die alttestamentliche Wissenschaft* 127 (2015): 716–13.

For Further Reading

Glatzer, Nahum N. *The Dimensions of Job*. New York: Schocken, 1969.

Larrimore, Mark. *The Book of Job: A Biography*. Princeton: Princeton University Press, 2013.

Terrien, Samuel. *The Iconography of Job through the Centuries*. University Park, PA: Penn State Press, 1996.

Vicchio, Stephen J. *Job in the Ancient World*. Eugene, OR: Wipf and Stock, 2006.

———. *Job in the Medieval World*. Eugene, OR: Wipf and Stock, 2006.

———. *Job in the Modern World*. Eugene, OR: Wipf and Stock, 2006.

Index

Adam, 132, 164
Akkadian, 4, 8, 17, 28, 36, 57, 106, 122, 125, 163, 170, 173. *See also* Assyrian, Old; Babylonian
Alalakh, 27, 40
Allusion, xxi, xxx, xxxiv, 30, 39, 42, 60, 66, 67, 68, 69, 73, 74, 78, 79, 83, 85, 87, 96, 101, 106, 111, 120, 122, 123, 130, 131, 139, 146, 147, 150, 151, 161, 184. *See also* Parody
Ambiguity, 9, 20, 27, 116, 137, 155, 186. *See also* Polysemy
Angels, 3, 5, 7, 17, 28, 66, 141, 167
Aqhat epic, xxiii–xxiv
Arabic, xiv, xxvii, 13, 14, 17, 18, 45, 57, 68, 83, 105, 112, 126, 150, 158, 169, 173, 178, 182, 184, 188
Aramaic, xxvii, 19–20, 24, 37, 59, 60, 73, 75, 85, 87, 95, 101, 108, 109, 111, 115, 120, 140, 144, 152, 154, 155, 156, 157, 158, 178, 179, 182; pseudo-Aramaic 28, 37, 126, 156; Samaritan, 179; translation, xviii, xxxi, 94, 115, 132. *See also* Qumran Aramaic translation
Assyrian, Old, 180

Attention, divine, 30
Ayyabu, xxiii, 4

Babylonian, xxvii, xxix, 22, 68, 71, 85, 86, 116; *Enuma Elish*, 116; hymn to Shamash, 161; "I Shall Praise the Lord of Wisdom," 16, 63, 74, 85; 'Theodicy, xxi
Beccuin, 125
Behemoth, 28, 52, 177–78
Behistun inscription, 86
Blasphemy, xviii, xxiv, 34
Boils, plague of, 9–10
Borshe the Silent, xxi
Book of the Dead (Egyptian), 121
Borrowing: linguistic, 17, 22, 36, 68; literary, 39. *See also* Allusion
Buber, Martin, and Franz Rosenzweig, method of, xxxvi

Chaldeans, 7
Constellations, 39, 170
Curse, xxiv, xxvi, xxxvii, 3, 5, 12, 13, 14, 21, 58, 78, 80, 110, 111, 118, 123, 132, 186
Cush, 163

Index

Danel, xxiii–xxiv
Darius, 86
Date of Job, xxvii
Day of the Lord, 107
Dead, realm of, 46, 48, 59, 61–62, 76,
    114, 115, 160, 164, 168
Death, 12, 24, 35, 38, 61, 74, 79–80,
    88, 96, 119, 140, 146, 172. *See also*
    Dead, realm of
Deep, the, 163, 168, 169
Defiance of Job, xx–xxi, 26
Demons, xvi, 24, 79–80, 87
Dialogue, xxx, xxxiii, xxxvii, 134–35,
    177; divine, 65
Difficulty in interpreting Job, ix, x,
    xxviii–xxxii, xxxv, 22, 49, 52, 107,
    110, 116, 168
Direct discourse. *See* Quotation and
    paraphrase; Speech
Discipline, divine, 19, 23–24, 26, 134,
    140, 152, 154, 175
Disputation, xxiv, 105
Divine assembly, 5, 17, 19, 26, 65
Double entendre. *See* Polysemy
Dust and ashes, xix–xx, 127, 185

Eavesdropping, 65
Echo, literary, 15, 17, 22, 29, 35, 48,
    50, 60, 61, 62, 66, 67, 68, 69, 71,
    72, 73, 77, 78, 89, 90, 102, 108,
    111, 112, 119, 136, 144, 154, 161,
    167, 180. *See also* Allusion
Edom, 4, 10, 80, 135
Egypt, 4, 55, 146, 177
Egyptian, xxi–xxii, 14, 36, 51, 170;
    Book of the Dead, 121; "Eloquent
    Peasant," xxi–xxii
El. *See* Names of God
Elihu chapters, xxv, xxxii, 47, 110,
    134–35, 160–61

Ellipsis, 83, 91, 105, 124
Eloah. *See* Names of God
Elohim. *See* Names of God
"Eloquent Peasant" (Egyptian), xxi–xxii
Enallage, 71, 167
Enuma Elish (Babylonian), 116
Epilogue, xxiv, 186
Epistemology, xxvi–xxvii
Epithet, divine, 122, 141, 159
Ethiopic, 31
Euphemism, 33, 178; "blessing" as,
    xxvi, 3, 5
Evil eye, 72

Fear of God, 4, 100
Figuration, xx, 4, 18, 68, 83, 90, 97,
    114, 115, 123, 126, 127, 129, 138,
    154, 157, 159, 168, 183, 185. *See
    also* Imagery; Metaphor
Folktale features, 3

Gesture, 11, 39, 40, 71, 74, 120, 122,
    131, 175
Gezer Calendar, 107
Gloss on text 31, 32, 49
Greek version, 10, 29, 41, 46, 67, 69,
    78, 80, 100, 102, 105, 106, 108,
    111, 119, 120, 143, 153, 163, 181.
    See also Translation: ancient
    translations of Job

Heart, as source of speech, 29, 36, 118
Hebrew, Late/Mishnaic/Rabbinic, 15,
    18, 25, 78, 103, 108, 156
Hebrew literary tradition, xxii–xxiii,
    xxviii
Hittite prayers, 43
Honest speech, xxv–xxvi, xxxv, 29, 30,
    117, 138, 186–87. *See also* Integrity
Hubur, River, 140

Index

Rhetoric, xxii, xxxi, xxxii, xxxiii, xxxiv, xxxvi, 36, 117, 121
Rhetorical question, xxii, xxxiv, 145
Rhythm of the text, xxxvi–xxxvii
Riddle, 36, 160

Sabeans, 7
Sarcasm, 62, 168
Satan, 3, 5, 6, 9, 72, 127, 186
Satire. See Parody
Scribal correction, 33, 41, 57, 101, 135, 146, 158
Scribal error, xxxii, 57, 67, 69, 100, 101, 107, 115, 116, 118, 119, 130, 141, 146, 153, 155, 157, 158, 162, 167, 172, 180, 182, 183
Script, Hebrew, 17, 18, 94. See also Ligature of letters *nw*; Scribal error
Semitic idiom, 85, 105, 138, 157
Shaddai. See Names of God
Shakespeare, xxviii, 174
Sheol. See Dead, realm of
Skin disease, 9, 31, 34, 72, 79, 85, 128, 186. See also Boils, plague of
Solomon, 4
Speech: dialectal, xxviii; introduction to, xxxiv, 36, 52, 66, 113–14, 119
Spelling, 52, 57, 114, 115, 141, 163, 167, 172, 182. See also *Ketib* (written text) and *Qere* (tradition of reading)
Stigma, xxx, 70, 72, 76, 82, 121
Storm god, 116, 157, 165
Structure, textual, xxi, xxiv, xxv, xxxiii, xxxvii, 7, 160
Styx, River, 140
Subversion of the conventional, xxii, 12, 30, 42, 44, 45, 53, 58, 83, 84, 85, 96, 115, 123

Suffering servant, xviii
Superstition, 79
Synonyms, 21, 71, 73, 75, 125, 126, 144, 155, 182, 183
Syntax, Hebrew, xxxvii, 9, 20, 49, 101, 107, 155, 180
Syriac, 35, 46, 89, 97, 105, 119, 120, 126, 139

Talmud, 20, 129
Ten Commandments, 108
Tenth plague, 146
Testing the love bond, 3, 186
Textual difficulty, ix, xxxi–xxxii, xxxv, 29, 31, 49, 50, 59, 67, 79, 87, 96, 101, 103, 108, 110, 113, 115, 118, 124, 126, 127, 145, 146, 147, 151, 153, 155, 158, 162, 168, 179, 183. See also Making sense of the text; Scribal correction; Scribal error
"Theodicy" (Babylonian), xxi. See also Just retribution
Theophany. See Revelation
Thot, 170
Throne of God, 115
Ti'amat, 116
Tradition, xxi–xxii, xxv–xxvi, 23, 24, 38, 51, 55, 67, 68, 77, 96, 136, 143, 187. See also Proverbial sayings
Transjordan, xv, xxii, xxiii, xxvii, xxviii, 3, 4
Translation: ancient translations of Job, xviii, xxxi–xxxii, xxxiii, 35, 43, 46, 55, 60, 89, 94, 95, 102, 105, 106, 107, 111, 112, 119, 122, 143, 145, 151; mistranslation, 64; rationale of, xvii–xviii, xxxv–xxxvii. See also Aramaic;